design & make
jewellery
using textile
techniques

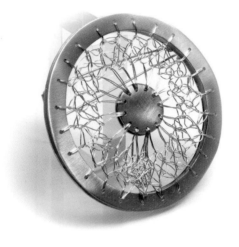

design & make

jewellery
using textile
techniques

SARAH KEAY

For my Mum and Dad

DISCLAIMER
Everything written in this book is to the best of my knowledge and every
effort has been made to ensure accuracy and safety but neither author nor
publisher can be held responsible for any resulting injury, damage or loss
to either persons or property. Any further information which will assist in
updating of any future editions would be gratefully received. Read through
all the information in each chapter before commencing work. Follow all
health and safety guidelines and where necessary obtain health and safety
information from the suppliers. Health and safety information can also be
found on the internet about certain products.

First published in Great Britain 2009
Bloomsbury Publishing Plc
50 Bedford Square
London WC1B 3DP
www.bloomsbury.com

739·27
1775406

Reprinted 2012

ISBN 978-1-4081-0107-0

Copyright © 2009 Sarah Keay

CIP catalogue records for this book are available
from the British Library and the US Library of Congress.

Sarah Keay has asserted her right under the
Copyright, Design and Patents Act, 1988, to be
identified as the author of this work.

Book design: Susan McIntyre
Cover design: Sutchinda Thompson
Commissioning editor: Susan James
Managing Editor: Sophie Page
Copy editor: Carol Waters

Printed and bound in China

Every effort has been made to ensure that all of the
information in this book is accurate. Due to differing
conditions, tools, materials and individual skills, the
publisher cannot be responsible for any injuries, losses
and other damages that may result from the use of the
information in this book.

Frontispiece image and image opposite, see p.43.

Contents

ACKNOWLEDGEMENTS

I would like to thank everyone who has helped in the making of this book.

To all the makers who kindly provided their time and energy to document and design the projects and who shared their processes so generously with us all: Vicky Forrester, Suzanne Smith, Liz Brown, Helen Robertson, Lilia Breyter, Sarah Kettley, Sarah Smith, Joanne Haywood, and to my own dearest mother whose crochet skills will always be beyond me. I couldn't have done it without all of your help and enthusiasm.

Many thanks also to all the makers whose images are included in this book and for all the many others who took the time to submit proposals, I wish I could have included more of you! All of your time is so very much appreciated.

To Rebecca van Rooijen of Benchpeg and Tina Rose of Craftscotland for their kind help in promoting the project, and finally to Sophie Page for all her editorial help and Susan James for her encouragement along the way and allowing me the opportunity to write about my passion.

1 introduction

Textile techniques are fantastic for showing individual expression, especially when combined with jewellery forms, materials and methods. There are so many ways in which to create beautiful pieces of jewellery, that don't require a lot of specialist equipment, or expensive materials. For anyone with an interest in making their own jewellery these methods make a great way to begin as they are very immediate and versatile and offer an endless variety of final outcomes.

Short historical and contextual backgrounds are included as these, with the techniques themselves, have driven my passion for the subject over the years. The projects themselves are supported by makers' work who have utilised those techniques within their practice and who have taken this media to a broad audience. These people have been chosen on a purely personal level as I am an admirer of the way in which they express their ideas and concepts.

It is my prime intention to provide as much information as I can for all the stages in the book and to offer a concise starting point for you to enjoy making jewellery using textile techniques. I hope that you find it as inspiring to use as I have writing it.

Sarah Keay, 2008

Green bangle by Sarah Keay, 2007. Enamelled wire, florist's wire, pearls, monofilament, enamel. Photograph © Sarah Keay.

jewellery using textile techniques

The aim of this publication is to demonstrate how you can use textile techniques to manipulate metal, fabric and other materials to make your very own wearable items of jewellery.

The book describes in depth how to apply textile techniques to both precious and non-precious materials, and allows for further experimentation within the subject.

Step-by-step projects sit alongside the historical application of the technique and ideas on how to develop your own original work using methods that date back to ancient cultures. It also describes in detail the necessary tools and materials required to make the piece together with tips to help you overcome any problems that may occur.

The well-illustrated techniques are demonstrated by examples of work by accomplished contemporary designers within the field today. This is to showcase the unique creations that can be achieved

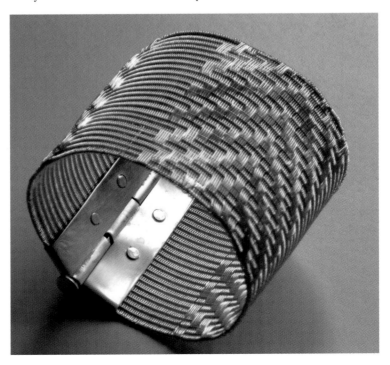

Bracelet by Lilia Breyter, 2007.
Sterling silver and fine silver.
Photograph © Paula Breyter.

by combining textile techniques with jewellery, enhancing the work of both jewellers and textile artists. This concept has been adopted by many weavers, basket makers and a whole host of other media artists, incorporating traditional jewellery orientated materials within their work.

There are also new techniques for utilising everyday materials such as paper and scraps of fabric, plus information on how to recycle old materials to transform them into stylish, wearable pieces of jewellery.

Many techniques can be achieved with limited tools. For instance knitting and crochet are simple to learn and have the advantage that they can be produced almost anywhere, even when travelling on a bus or the Underground. Other techniques such as bobbin lace and weaving are more difficult as they require specialist equipment and are not easily moved yet the outcome for all the techniques will leave you feeling very impressed, and hopefully wanting to learn more. With enough patience and ingenuity, most textile methods can be used on metals and other surprising materials and incorporated into scores of original designs and patterns.

Crystal bangle by Sarah Keay, 2007. Silver wire, rose quartz beads, swarovski crystals, monofilament, enamel. Photograph © Sarah Keay.

JEWELLERY USING TEXTILE TECHNIQUES

Knitted neckpiece by Rebajane, 2007.
Sterling silver, gold metallic thread.
Photograph © Stephen Bonser.

All the processes are deliberately developed to give directions for makers to begin experimenting with the technique themselves, in order to inspire their own designs and creations. If more information is required the reader can look through the bibliography and suppliers list to find further sources of information on the subject.

I would just like to note here that although most of the processes are not in any way dangerous please take care when making these projects as accidents can happen! For instance when using wire be careful to watch the ends, or, as I do, wear safety goggles. With many of these projects your attention and focus will be on the actual work, not what's going on around you!

The finished pieces have a multitude of possibilities for those who wish to experiment with the scale of the piece, or combine it with any other material or technique. Lastly there is no right or wrong way for these techniques to be used. It is entirely up to the maker to choose which direction to take!

history of the crossover between jewellery and textile techniques

The wearing of jewellery has been a constant feature throughout human existence. Amongst scattered cultures, the same desire to adorn their bodies is evident, with each one of them developing a truly unique style.

By 30,000 BC, hunters from across Europe were making items of jewellery using natural materials, such as skins, bone, teeth, seeds and berries, and wearing them not only as amulets but also as decoration. Over the years the techniques of manipulating materials grew and experiments with forms and textures evolved into the body adornment of today.

Jewellery was initially created for practical uses such as pinning clothes together and as a display of wealth. More recently it has been used almost exclusively as a form of decoration.

Jewellery's uses throughout history have been predominantly:
▶ Currency, and as a display of wealth,
▶ Functional, such as clasps and pins,
▶ Symbolism,
▶ Protection, in the forms of amulets,
▶ Self expression.

The crossover between jewellery and textiles is certainly not a new one. There have been examples throughout history ranging from pre-Colombian textiles right the way through to contemporary makers. In medieval Europe alongside elaborate lace work there are rich embroideries using metal coated thread. The thread would often be manufactured by winding incredibly fine wire around silk or linen thread. It would then be used to decorate items ranging from Royal garments to large-scale tapestries.

The concept of hand stitching metal and found objects onto fabrics can be found in many locations and time periods. This is the simplest of techniques and the sewing of such objects, such as mirrors, onto fabrics is evident in many cultures even today.

Mirrors are used to warn away evil or the use of red thread is thought to give the item its protective power.

AMULETIC PROPERTIES

"An amulet is an object that is designed to bring good luck or protect the wearer from trouble". The role of jewellery in the West is usually as a display of wealth, with a few exceptions – the wedding ring and religious pendants, for example. However in many parts of the world jewellery is often worn for its amuletic power. The protective powers of precious and semi-precious stones and other materials determine the final item of jewellery. For this reason, in contrast to the West, where we keep certain items of jewellery for special occasions, because of this symbolism, amuletic jewellery is everyday wear.

BEADS

Beads are of ancient origin. Throughout the early periods of Egypt, the Mediterranean and Western Asia, beads acted as a status symbol but were also used as amulets usually by being stitched onto clothes, where the colour was the defining power. Beads were also hand sewn onto weavings and embroideries to attract good spirits.

THREAD

Threads can be woven, stitched and dyed in ways to keep away evil spirits, they can also be twisted, knotted and tangled up to trap the spirits. The simple method of tying a knot of thread is universal. In the Graeco-Roman world the 'Hercules' knot was a design of amuletic jewellery.

PEARLS

Today the European bridal veil derives from the pearl headdresses that used to be worn to frighten away the evil eye. The lustre of pearls and its ability to reflect light was thought to scare away the evil eye on the bride's wedding day. Today in the Nasaud region of Northern Romania, bridal headdresses are still made incorporating pearls and mirrors for this very reason. Today these materials are mixed with crepe paper and tin foil to form the headdresses.

NATIVE AMERICAN JEWELLERY

The Native Americans have been producing jewellery since ancient times. A bracelet, which dates to around AD 800, has been found that was made using basketry techniques. For decoration, it has been encrusted with turquoise plaques and glued using pine pitch adhesive.

BEADWORK

From around 1900, Apache women were making a variety of woven neck pieces from seed beads, including shawl collars and T-necklaces. The Yuma tribes of the Mojave, had begun creating seed bead netted collars, using a needle and thread and stringing multiple beads at once, a technique which later spread to other tribes. For example there are beautiful Choctaw bandolier sashes from around 1907 that are produced with embroidered beadwork in complex scroll designs.

FOUND OBJECTS

The Native Americans were superb at utilising the natural resources that were available to them. There are examples of necklaces of strung plaited buckskin, which include eagle talons, bird feet, dewclaws, buffalo horn, brass thimbles, bells, glass beads and ribbons. The pieces show great creativity using such objects.

QUILLWORK

Quillwork medallions have been found that are dyed with local plant juices, goldenrod and blueberry for instance, that are then suspended from a bone and glass bead necklace. The Yukon made necklaces constructed from aboriginal caribou hide with quill embroidery, decorated with imported glass beads, buttons and clock springs.

JEWELLERY USING TEXTILE TECHNIQUES

the beginning of contemporary jewellery using textile techniques

Historical examples of items combining metal and textile techniques can be found within very different times and countries, from ancient Greece and medieval Europe to tribal decoration in Africa. What is surprising is how little they have in common, occurring apparently randomly with isolated techniques.

The large majority of items seem mainly to have been produced for ceremonial occasions as they are so richly decorated. However, there are more subtle pieces; such as the tubes of spiraled wire sewn into fabrics that derive from Finland around AD 1200.

There is also the recurring practice of embellishing metals with fabric-like motifs or decorating the surface of metals with textile motifs such as twisting, braiding and filigree patterns.

Over the last 40 years there has been a renewed interest in the application of textile methods in modern jewellery. The reworking of the ordinary, almost mundane, has produced some of the most innovative and compelling pieces of work not only in the fields of textiles and jewellery but also in fine art. The traditional boundaries have been challenged and the result has led to a far more fluid and interdisciplinary way of creating. This has also led to the use of far less conventional materials. Monofilament, wool and copper wire have been chosen not only to challenge the traditional preconceptions of jewellery but also the intrinsic value of the finished work. Wool, yarn and wire are all inexpensive yet highly versatile materials. They can be plaited, knotted, wrapped, coiled or twisted.

Many makers choose to combine jewellery and textile techniques, as demonstrated by the American jeweller knitting large-scale collars in 1975 to the Dutch maker in 2008 who incorporates delicately crocheted units with found objects to make quirky necklaces and rings. Makers from decades ago to the present day use the same techniques, to experiment with the vast array of possibilities that these techniques provide. Using these techniques doesn't constitute a style or movement; it purely demonstrates how limitless the crossover can be.

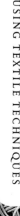

Today many examples of the use of metal in textile structures can be found in mass-produced materials such as industrial copper tubing, used as jackets for building cables.

contemporary combinations of jewellery and textile techniques

Textile techniques such as knitting, crochet and weaving have been adapted by jewellers for items made with precious materials. Below is a list of my own personal favourites that have inspired me.

jewellery

ARLINE FISCH

Arline Fisch can be seen as one of the true pioneers of jewellery using textile techniques, contributing unique and personal creations to the area of body adornment. Through her work and her teaching she has created a platform for other makers to experiment. She is an internationally known artist who applies the structures and techniques of fabric to precious and non-precious metals, creating intricate, colourful jewellery by knitting, crocheting, plaiting and weaving. She is also the author of the definitive book in the field, *Textile Techniques in Metal*.

CAROLINE BROADHEAD

Caroline Broadhead's work crosses over the areas of jewellery, textiles and performance art. In her early work she made nylon monofilament structures that could be collapsed to form neckpieces or pulled up to form a ruff effect or even expanded to cover the face and head. She also used multi-coloured woven flax for broad hooped necklaces and bracelets. In 1986 she produced large body garments including *Cocoon* and *Seam*. Since then she has continued to cross boundaries with her work. In 1997, she won the *Jerwood Prize for Applied Arts: Textiles*.

CATHERINE MARTIN

Catherine Martin has adapted the traditional Japanese braiding technique of kumihimo into her braided wire forms using precious materials. Recent work includes delicately shading platinum into rich golds.

FELIEKE VAN DER LEEST

Felieke van der Leest combines found objects, such as plastic toy animals, crochet work, gold and silver into her pieces of jewellery. She meticulously crochets viscose and cotton for her animals to wear, which then dangle from crocheted chain necklaces. She also sets precious stones such as topaz or ruby into their eyes, to represent the joy that she has in making the work.

FLORA BOOK

Flora Book's ornamental body pieces cross the boundaries between garments and jewellery. She experiments with hard materials such as silver and glass and turns them into flexible fabrics by weaving them with nylon. She also knits and felts with silver and glass.

MARY LEE HU

Mary Lee Hu is famous for her development in weaving using fine gauge wire. By using just one colour, interest and texture is added through the pattern of the weave. She weaves with 18ct and 22ct gold wires, using multiple strand warps and wefts.

NORA FOK

Nora Fok is a maker of wearable sculptural objects in which her principle material is nylon monofilament. Occasionally she incorporates plastics and other materials into the pieces. Her techniques involve knitting, knotting, tying and weaving.

SUSAN CROSS

Susan Cross is the recent joint winner of the *Jerwood Jewellery Prize*. She works primarily in precious metals using constructed textile techniques. She has used methods including braiding, binding, wrapping and crochet.

fine art

MONA HATOUM

One of the clearest uses of allegory in contemporary fine art is by Mona Hatoum. In her 1995, *Hair Necklace*, she displays a work of intricately woven balls made from her own brown hair and strung together. The piece went on display on a bust in a booth at the Cartier shop in Bordeaux. One of the most symbolic materials is hair. Here Hatoum drew from a variety of connotations, ranging from the more recent historical use of hair as a symbol of love, from the eighteenth century *momento mori* to the primal use of hair as a mark of identity. The glamour and elegance that the Cartier name carries directly contradicts the monetary value of a commodity such as discarded hair.

textiles

DEIRDRE NELSON

Deirdre Nelson is one of Britain's leading contemporary textile artists. Deirdre's *What lies beneath* series studies the stories of traditional needlework crafts and offers a fascinating view into the history of knitting and embroidery through memories, facts and anecdotes. The role of knitting in traditional bartering systems informs many of the pieces. *Thimbleknocking*, is an example which, on first appearance, is just a pair of Victorian bloomers, however the thimble belt embellishment, handstitched by the artist, acts as a reminder that many of the young women employed in the needlework industry had to supplement their meagre incomes by succumbing to prostitution; the thimbles being used to tap on windows to lure potential customers.

Distressed thimbles by Deirdre Nelson, 2007. Found thimbles, pierced. Photograph © Tony Nathan.

gallery – susan cross

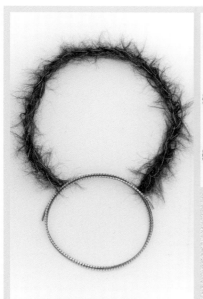

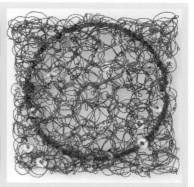

CLOCKWISE FROM ABOVE
Brooch, 2005. Oxidised silver, thread.

Brooch, 2007. Oxidised silver, 18ct gold.
7.5 x 7.5 cm (3 x 3 in.).

Neckpiece, 2005. Oxidised silver.
40 cm (16 in.) length.

Neckpiece, 2005. Oxidised silver, thread.
45 cm (18 in.) length.

Neckpiece, 2008. Oxidised silver, 17ct gold,
stainless steel. 10 x 11 cm (4 x 4.3 in.).

Photographs © Joël Degen and John K
McGregor.

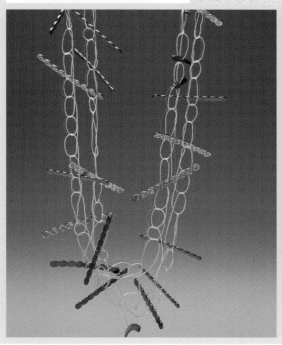

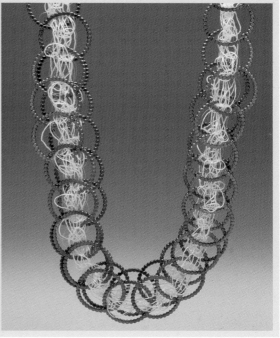

embroidery – helene turbe

"The main source of inspiration for my work comes from religious icons. I'm fascinated by the peace and the beauty which emanates from them.

I love to challenge the materials I use as I love to play with their opposites; the wrong side of an embroidery, the crack of the enamel, the quirky and the beauty, the sadness and the innocence, the disturbing and the fascinating ...

I hope to think that my pieces tell a story, evoke the same emotion to people as they evoke to me when I make them.

My work is just the starting point, the past and the future belong to people's own imagination, own sensitivity."
Helene Turbe 2008

CLOCKWISE FROM TOP LEFT
Pinocchi' Owl, 2007. Totem made with wood, threads. Brooch made with silver, enamel.

Brooch, Rabbit (detail), 2005. Silver, silver chain, fabric, stiching, and antique buttons.

Angel with a broken arm, 2007. Totem made with wood, fabric. Brooch made with silver, pin-ball.

A Mon Enfant. Sculpture, 2007. Wood, fabric, steel wire, pin-ball.

Photographs © Helene Turbe.

2 before you begin

materials

Most textile techniques involve a lot of looping over, interlacing or friction to achieve the right tension and strength. Crochet cotton, yarn, string or thread are the easiest materials to work with and ones that I would suggest you use to try practice pieces before starting with any specialist or expensive materials such as silver wire.

When working with less malleable materials such as wire, always be aware of the tendency for it to break or snap if pulled or stretched too tight! Also when designing your own jewellery remember that certain materials only work well with certain techniques, for instance wire that you can knit with may not be strong enough to endure the tension required for weaving and vice versa. Trial and error is a must.

When I talk about malleability I'm referring to the length of time and the amount of manipulation that can occur before it will break. The most forgiving material is 24ct gold. It can be stretched, twisted and folded almost infinitely. However for the purpose of this book it can be too soft to hold the structure up. In my experience when gold is required, I start with a layer of around 0.3–0.5 mm (0.01–0.02 in.) gold plated silver wire to add the necessary strength to be durable enough to wear everyday. On the other side of the scale are the base metals, which are unsuitable for most textile techniques as they are so brittle and will snap under the least amount of tension. By contacting the suppliers with such questions most projects can be achieved.

In between these two extremes lie every other possible material to work with.

Some materials will break instantly when put under pressure, others will slowly weaken as the process continues. Others may not keep their shape and the instant that they are unpinned from the work surface may spring into another unintended shape. Generally it is the thickness of the wire itself that is the most important aspect in determining which material is suited to which technique. Most of the techniques covered in this book work with the thinner range of wires as these are the most flexible. Anywhere between 0.2–0.5mm (0.007–0.02 in.) is perfect for most techniques. As the size goes up, 1 mm (0.04 in.) and above, the flexibility of the wire decreases and the strength required to manipulate it is increased. Recently I started using 1 mm (0.04 in.) for my knitted projects and within a few weeks I started to experience severe pains in my hands. Since then I've found that it is easier to layer up thinner wires to achieve the density that my designs required.

You should not experience any pain in making any of these projects. If you do please work with thinner materials. These projects are meant to be enjoyed, not endured!

Gold, silver, copper and enamelled wire are all easy enough to work with even without tools in many cases.

Another crucial point to mention before beginning is that in many techniques, such as crochet and knitting, a continuous length of wire is vital as it avoids the problem of joining two ends neatly within the design. Most wire comes on spools. If your wire arrives in a coil it is a good idea to transfer it onto a spool or even a piece of cardboard before beginning, as once the wire is uncoiled it can wrap itself up into a spring which can be a nightmare to untangle, especially when half way through a complicated project. If not spooled up it is also liable to kink in places, which can detract from the design but also weakens the wire. This can lead to it breaking if any pressure is put on it when it is worn.

If you wish to change the look of the piece an easy way is to roll down the wire to make thin strips that can then be woven, bound, etc. This can be done easily with a rolling mill, or if you want it to look handmade or slightly uneven, you can hammer the wire on a steel block. This may be more tricky when you need to work with a long length. In this case it is easier to have two spools working, one with the round wire and the other for the hammered wire with the steel block in between, with both constantly revolving to keep the wire as controlled as possible. Some cloisonné wire may also be used as it is a thin, flat wire. As it is very time consuming to draw wire down to the correct length and size and you need a lot of specialised equipment, I recommend buying it pre-annealed and spooled. Therefore when it arrives work can begin immediately.

SILVER

The two common types of silver mentioned are fine silver and sterling silver. Techniques such as knitting, crochet and lace are easier made using fine silver as it can be manipulated into quite complicated designs without showing any signs of weakness. Sterling silver on the other hand is far better at holding its shape; however, it can respond badly to constant working and can fracture and break.

Sterling silver is most commonly used due to its strength but is most suited to techniques such as weaving where there is only the minimum of stress put on the wire.

Sterling silver is also more readily available in a wide range of sizes, whereas fine silver tends to be more available in finer sizes. Sterling can also be bought more widely in strip form. Spools can be easily purchased from 50 g (1.7 oz) right up to 500 g (17.5 oz) and beyond.

COPPER

Copper wire is the most accessible wire and also the cheapest and is just as flexible as fine silver. It can be used in most textile techniques as it can withstand a lot of manipulation. It can also be recycled as very fine copper is used in circuit boards, machinery and a multitude of other commercial items.

TIP

❝ If your wire is not on a spool, e.g. as a coil, then transfer it onto an old spool or piece of cardboard . ❞

TOOLS REQUIRED

▸ **Scissors** – paper cutting scissors are more than satisfactory for cutting wire of 1 mm (0.04 in.) and less.

▸ **Wire Cutters** – these can be used to cut wire and are essential for wire that is above 1 mm (0.04 in.).

▸ **Jewellers pliers** – are better for using in these projects as they don't have serrated plates and are less damaging to the wire, especially coated wires. These pliers come in a variety of shapes for different uses such as:

Round-nose – essential for textile techniques as they are used to coil the ends of the wire to neaten up the finished design.

Flat-nose – another good set of pliers to have as these can flatten out any small kinks that appear in the wire as you are working with it.

▸ **Files** – are used for smoothing off the ends of wire. Hand files can be sourced from a variety of shops, but remember the more expensive they are the better quality they will be.

Flat-edged files are probably the most useful file to buy although they are usually for sale in packs with round and square files also included.

▸ **Tweezers** – these can be the regular shop bought variety or a specialist jewellers set. They are great for working with small units, such as seed beads, and can also be used to hold or move wires with minimum disruption to surrounding parts.

finishing off

With all the textile techniques covered in this book, the endings will need to be very well thought out. One way would be to make your own from either textile techniques themselves such as braiding, or heavier units made from sheet silver. The latter can be learned through the books in the bibliography.

If you have access to metalworking tools and equipment and have a good knowledge of the basic techniques, you could make your own using the materials that you have available. The simplest way to finish the ends where there are multiple wires, especially woven pieces, is to take a rectangle of silver, or any other suitable metal, the same width as the textile. Score a line down the centre then fold it over onto itself catching all the wires in the fold. Flatten it down with a mallet or anything heavy. File the edges and polish or texture with sandpaper, steel wool or however else you wish.

Other techniques include riveting and beading which can be easily learned and require the minimum amount of tools and equipment.

The endings should be both compatible with the overall design and the movement of the piece. Too heavy an end could be disastrous if the design is made from fine wire, the opposite is also true as the catch needs to be stout enough if the finished piece is quite heavy.

3 felt

Felt is a non-woven cloth that is produced by matting, shrinking and pressing fibres. While some types of felt are very soft, it can be thick and strong enough to use as a construction material for structures such as yurts. Felt is one of the oldest forms of fabric known and certainly predates weaving and knitting. In Turkey alone, the remains of felt have been found dating as far back as 6,500 BC.

felt brooch by suzanne smith

EQUIPMENT REQUIRED

- bamboo mat (e.g. old blind, sushi mat)
- bubble wrap
- old towels (to soak up excess water/protect surface)
- spray bottle able to withstand boiling water (e.g. plant water spray)
- soap flakes
- hot water
- apron if required
- rubber gloves if required
- plastic carrier bag
- scissors
- needle and thread

MATERIALS REQUIRED

- dyed merino wool tops in desired colours (x3 shades)
- glass seed beads
- brooch fitting
- pen and paper
- 1 sheet shop bought felt

method

step 1 layout

Place a towel on the table, followed by the bamboo mat then the bubblewrap. Tease out small tufts of wool, 8–10 cm (3–4 in.) approx. and lay out on the mat with the fibres running horizontally.

Repeat this step to make another layer but lay out the wool vertically i.e. with the fibres at right angles to the previous layer.

A rough guideline is that an A4 sized wool layer will felt into an A5 sheet, with enough hot water, friction and heat.

Make a soap solution by pouring some boiling water into the spray bottle and adding 2-3 pinches of soap flakes. Shake well to mix.

step 2 felt shapes

a. Soak the prepared wool (prefelt) thoroughly, including the edges.

b. Scrunch the plastic bag in your hand and rub in a circular motion for a few minutes until the wool flattens.

c. Wrap the bubblewrap over the felt and then roll the mat into a sausage shape.

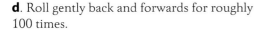

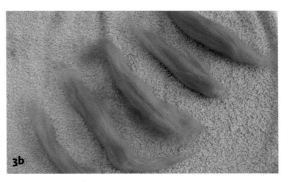

d. Roll gently back and forwards for roughly 100 times.

Unroll the mat and bubblewrap, then turn the prefelt 90 degrees and soak again with hot soap solution.

Repeat this process, remembering to change the direction of the prefelt every 100 rolls, continuing until the fibres are sufficiently felted.

There should be no movement of the fibres and the sheet should be a smaller and denser fabric.

Rinse out in cold water and squeeze any excess liquid out. Allow to dry overnight on a radiator.

Start the process again with the next colour.

step 3 felt ball
a. **b**. Tease off 5 small tufts of prefelt.

c. Wrap one tuft around your finger tightly.

d. Wrap the second tuft around the first layer, folding over the edges to make a rectangular form. Repeat for all the remaining tufts.

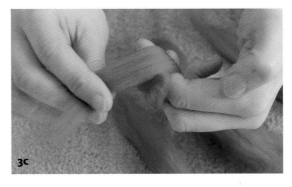

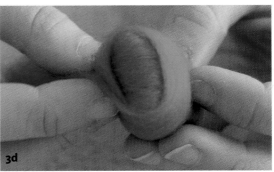

3e

3f

e. Spray the surface of the ball with soap solution, focusing especially on any overlapping areas. Gently rub overlaps to start with on both sides.

f. Form ball by rolling between your palms in a circular motion until the ball has felted and is firm to the touch. Rinse and allow to dry.

step 4 cut out shapes from felt made in step 2

Use a paper or acetate template if necessary.

a. With a sharp pair of scissors cut out two leaves.

b. Cut out five petals.

c. Cut out two smaller leaves with the shop bought felt.

TIP

❝ Pinking shears can add lovely texture and interest to the piece if desired. ❞

4a

4b

4c

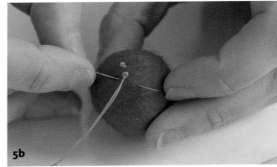

step 5 sew together

a. Stitch together the petals at the centre point.

b. Next sew some randomly spaced seed beads onto the ball. Attach the ball to the centre of the flower.

For the leaves either machine or handsew down the centre of each leaf.

c. Sew together leaves and brooch clasp onto the back of the flower.

Suzanne can be contacted by
e-mail: hello@suzannesmithdesign.co.uk
Website: www.suzanne-smith.co.uk
Project photographs © Sarah Keay.

The finished brooch.

nuno felt

FACT

66 Nuno felting is a Japanese felting technique. It bonds loose fibres, usually wool, into a sheer fabric such as silk chiffon, as in this project. This creates a lightweight felt that can completely cover the background fabric or it can be used as a single decorative design.

The Nuno felting process is particularly suited to very fine items, since the silk-backing ensures a stable fabric that won't stretch out of shape like normal felt. Also as it is so lightweight and easy to manipulate, it can be dyed more easily than traditional felt. Other fabrics can be used as the felting background, resulting in a huge variety of textural effects. 99

JEWELLERY USING TEXTILE TECHNIQUES

autumnal felt necklace
by liz brown

EQUIPMENT REQUIRED

- bamboo mat (e.g. old blind, sushi mat)
- bubble wrap and old towels (to protect surface/soak up excess water)
- spray bottle able to withstand boiling water (e.g. plant water spray)
- soap flakes
- hot water
- apron if required
- plastic carrier bag
- rubber gloves if required
- scissors
- pen and paper
- needle and thread

MATERIALS REQUIRED

- dyed merino wool tops in desired colours
- angelina fibre
- silk cocoons
- silk chiffon
- 7-strand satin coated cable wire
- cullote open crimp bead
- crimp beads
- glass seed beads
- necklace clasp

method

step 1 for all wool leaves

Lay out very thinly 2–3 wispy layers of wool, varying the colours and varieties. Fine wisps of angelina heat-bondable fibre are then laid onto the surface for a shimmer effect, together with the silk fibres.

For the Nuno felt leaves, in this design the green and brown leaves, lay out the felt onto the white silk chiffon to add texture and strength.

step 2 start to felt

Cover the wool with a man-made material such as nylon netting or bubblewrap. Add warm water with a little soap solution and push down gently on the surface of the net to flatten the wool, use a little soap on the surface and rub gently in circles becoming increasingly firmer as the fibres flatten.

Once all the wool is flat turn the whole thing over and repeat the process. You may be firmer with this side as the pattern is not easily moved at this stage. Because the layers are so fine they will felt together very quickly.

Turn back over to the front and lift the net to check that the design has not moved. If it has it can be easily nudged gently back into place.

Replace the net and rub more harshly.

Your wool has now become a fabric and will just about hold together but it needs to be fulled (shrunk and hardened) to be suitable for the purpose of wearing it as a piece of jewellery.

TIP

❝ For the chiffon you could reuse an old scarf that you have lying around or an old chiffon shirt! ❞

step 3 fulling

This can be done by rolling the net parcel in a bamboo mat or blind. Remember to continually change the direction that the felt lies on in the mat after a set amount of rolls. 25 is a good number to work with. Generally after the first 25 rolls the net can be removed and the rolling done directly in the blind.

The fulling can also be done in the hand by warming the piece of felt in water and rolling in the hand to a number of counts (try 5 to begin with) remember to unfold and straighten after each roll or it will felt into itself. The piece of felt will shrink considerably depending on the variety of wool and the thickness of the layers. Rinse out the soap when finished and iron, (remembering to cover the surface to protect the angelina fibres). Allow to dry.

FACT: FULLING

❝ Fulling is also called 'felting' or 'boiled wool' by many makers. You can create your own fulled or felted fabric at home by placing an old jumper in a washing machine set on hot, with the usual amount of washing powder. The heat, water and movement makes the fibres bond together. The condensed end result is a dense and durable fabric. Most woollen items and almost any animal hair will felt easily, however cotton, acrylics and synthetics will not. ❞

step 4 leaf template

Plan your template shapes for the leaves. A good idea is to use a sheet of clear acetate or paper as it will allow you to position your shape over the best surface design. Draw around and cut out. Repeat until you have the desired number.

step 5 stiffen leaves

Once cut out, a solution of water-based millenary hat stiffener is used. 1 part stiffener to 4 parts water is generally the best. PVA can also be diluted to the same consistency however it may leave the surface a bit shiny. Dip the leaves individually into the solution, squeeze out the excess liquid and allow to dry.

step 6 silk cocoons

Prepare the cut silk cocoons. These also need to be stiffened as above as they will not be robust enough to wear otherwise. Once dry pierce a hole with a sharp needle or fine awl but from the inside out to avoid denting the surface. The cocoons can be coloured with wool dyes or purchased ready dyed.

SILK FACTS

“ Every silk cocoon has approximately 1 kilometre (1000 yards) of silk filament, when drawn out in a line.

In 2007, archaeologists found woven and dyed silk fabrics in a tomb in China that were about 2,500 years old.

Silk is one of the toughest natural fibres but can lose up to 20% of its strength when wet. ”

step 7 finishing off

Lay out your pattern on a flat surface. Using the 7-strand satin coated cable wire, attach the correct length to the end of the fastener using crimp beads.

Each of the 3 lengths should differ, and remember to allow extra for gathering of fabrics.

Choose the glass beads to fill the wire between your leaves and cocoons. Contrasting colours work as well as blended colour shades.

a. Your felted leaves are threaded onto the cable by piercing a double hole on the back of the leaf horizontally. Try to run the hole and cable through the fibres so that the bare cable is not visible from the front or thread some beads on it to make a feature of it. Space your pieces so no two leaves or cocoons are lying directly next to one another.

b. Complete the rows one by one and seal the beads on each end by crimping and securing before beginning the next line. When all 3 rows are wired and secured you can use the cullote open crimp bead to secure the cables together in the design of your choice.

Try on the body first as your placement will dictate how the finished item will 'sit' on the wearer. Enjoy!

7a

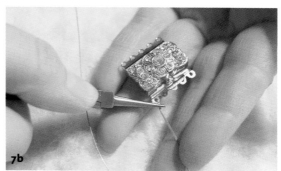

7b

Liz can be contacted by:
telephone: 01290 700437
e-mail: info@heartfeltbyliz.com
Project photographs © Sarah Keay.

Finished felt necklace. Photograph © Liz Brown.

gallery – suzanne smith

ABOVE *Candy rings* by Suzanne Smith, 2007. Oxidised white metal, handmade felt, dyed lace, mother of pearl. The *Candy rings* are handmade felt that is covered with hand dyed lace and finished with lace flowers sewn onto the surface. The felt is then attached to the oxidised white metal ring.

RIGHT, TOP *Flower Ball necklace*, 2007. Oxidised white metal chain, handmade felt, dyed lace flowers and glass beads.
For this piece the felt ball was made by hand using the wet felting technique. The hand dyed lace flowers are then hand stitched onto the surface before it is attached to the chain.

RIGHT *Oval Flower brooch*, 2007. Oxidised white metal, handmade felt, dyed lace, leather, embroidery threads. Roll printed white metal brooch, filled with handmade lace which has been bonded with the dyed lace. The brooch is then decorated with embroidery threads, dyed lace flowers and leather leaves.

Photographs © Suzanne Smith.

natalya pinchuk

"Time after time, my decisions in the studio bring me to bold and large-scale jewellery. It is perhaps because I desire to activate the body and make the wearer along with passer-bys acknowledge the body as a changing and shifting organism with things growing within it. I enjoy observing that which puts me at awe and scares me, inevitably influencing my making. Snakes, lizards, insects, fungi, wilting flowers and decomposing fruit become my source material that I observe but do not copy. I want these necklaces to be attractive and lively, yet leaving a slight unsettling effect." Natalya Pinchuk 2008

TOP LEFT *Necklace. Growth Series.* 2007. Wool, copper, enamel, plastic, waxed thread, stainless steel, 45 cm (17.7 in.) long. Courtesy of Charon Kransen Arts.

TOP CENTRE *Necklace. Growth Series*, 2007. Wool, copper, enamel, plastic, leather, waxed thread, 44 cm (17.3 in.) long. Courtesy of Charon Kransen Arts.

TOP RIGHT AND DETAIL, RIGHT *Necklace. Growth Series.* 2007. Wool, copper, enamel, plastic, waxed thread, stainless steel, 76 cm (30 in.) long. Courtesy of Rob Koudijs Galerie.

Photographs © Natalya Pinchuk.

4 crochet

Crochet is a process of creating a fabric from yarn or thread using a crochet hook. The name derives from the old French word *croc* or *croche*, meaning hook. Crocheting, which is similar to knitting, consists of pulling loops of yarn through other loops. Crochet however differs from knitting in that only one loop is active at one time and that a crochet hook is used instead of knitting needles. The earliest written reference to crochet refers to shepherds knitting from *The Memoirs of a Highland Lady* by Elizabeth Grant in 1812.

crocheted silk necklace by marjory keay

EQUIPMENT REQUIRED

► Crochet hook size 1.25

MATERIAL REQUIRED

► 2 x 50 g Debbie Bliss 100% Pure Silk

TIP

❝ The necklace pictured is made using the treble crochet stitch, however any stitch will do for this pattern. ❞

method

step 1 start chain stitch

To begin, make a slip loop several inches from the end of the silk, and slip onto the crochet hook. This counts as your first chain stitch.

TIP

❝ This is the basic step of crochet, and it can easily be mastered in a few moments. If you have never crocheted before, it is best to begin with a thick crochet hook and double knitting yarn. ❞

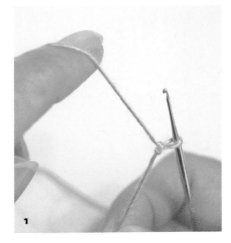

step 2 continue stitches

Continue making the length of chain stitches that you require, (300 in all for the necklace). Catch the silk with the crochet hook and pull it through the loop already on the hook.

step 3 create circle

Join up the first loop of the chain to the last loop to create a continuous circle.

step 4 treble crochet stitch

For the treble crochet stitch, pull the silk over the hook and draw a loop through the next stitch.

step 5 continue

Draw a loop through the first two loops on the hook, then draw another loop through the two remaining loops.

step 6 second row

Continue to do one treble stitch through each chain loop of the circle to create your second row.

step 7 third row

For your third row do two treble stitches into each loop of the circle.

step 8 fourth row

For the fourth row repeat step 7 by doing two treble stitches into each loop.

step 9 finishing off

When the circle is completed finish off the necklace. Thread the silk through the remaining loop using a needle.

8

9

The finished necklace. Project photographs © Sarah Keay.

JEWELLERY USING TEXTILE TECHNIQUES

gallery – tamara kronis

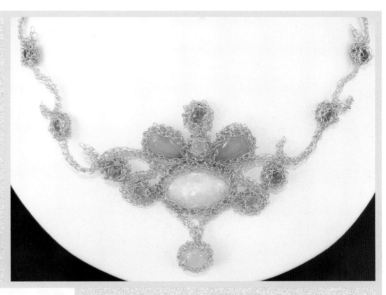

ABOVE *Art Nouveau necklace*, 2008. 18ct yellow gold and rubies, sapphires, garnets, amethysts, citrines, chalcedony, moonstones, a pearl, onyx and peridot.

LEFT *Crocheted ring*, 2007. Chalcedony and sterling silver.

BELOW *Crocheted bracelet*, 2008. 18ct yellow gold with lemon quartz, citrine, amethyst, garnet, peridot, black onyx and carnelian.

Photographs © Tamara Kronis.

christine kaltoft

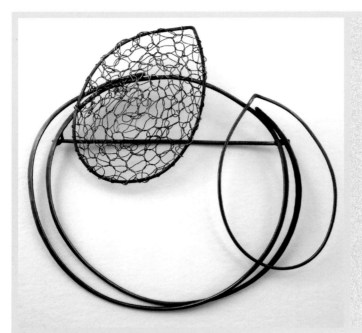

ABOVE *Chicken Legs brooch*, 2007. Oxidised silver. Framework of brooch forged and soldered. Panel of crocheted silver wire, with ends laser welded to stop unravelling.

RIGHT *Wired 1 brooch*. Steel and 18ct gold, finger crocheted and laser welded.

Photographs © Christine Kaltoft.

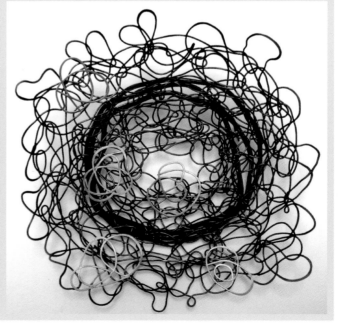

rebajane

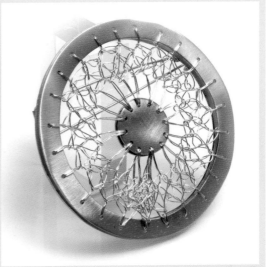

ABOVE *Pearl pendant*, 2007. Dyed pearls, gold metallic thread, fine silver wire. The tube for this pendant is made by crocheting the silver wire and thread together. The pearls are then strung inside the tube before the pendant is hung on the ribbon.

ABOVE RIGHT *Hairpin Lace brooch*, 2007. Silver.

RIGHT *Framed bracelet*, 2005. Silver, pearls.
For this piece Rebajane has knitted fine silver wire into rectangles using small needles, and randomly inserted the pearls. The knitted panels are strung onto the inside of the bracelet's framework.

Photographs © Stephen Bonser.

yael krakowski

CLOCKWISE FROM ABOVE

Cactus pendant, 2008. Silver, new jade, thread. 35 cm (13.7 in.) long.

Desert Flower necklace, 2008. Silver, carnelian, thread. 36 cm (14 in.) long

Ring, 2008. Silver, glass beads, thread. 4 x 5.5 cm (1.5 x 2 in.).

Soft Grenade pendant, 2005. Silver, carnelian, thread. 35 cm (13.7 in.) long.

Soft Grenade pendant, (detail), 2005.

Desert Flower necklace, 2008. Oxidised silver, carnelian, thread. 36 cm (14 in.) long.

Photographs © Yael Krakowski.

5 binding

silver bangle by vicky forrester

EQUIPMENT REQUIRED

► small round objects for forming the core wires – e.g. small bottle or jar
► steel rule
► snipe-nosed pliers
► wire cutters
► needle file for filing the core wire flush with tubing

MATERIALS REQUIRED

► radial wires: 7.5 m (24.5 ft) (soft sterling silver wire, 7 mm diameter
► core wires: 1 m (3 ft) hard sterling silver wire, 1 mm (0.04 in.) diameter
► 4 x sterling silver crimps (silver tubing with 1 mm (0.04 in.) internal diameter, cut to 5 mm (0.02 in.) lengths)
► superglue for securing the tubing
► masking tape to hold the core wires in a circle at the beginning

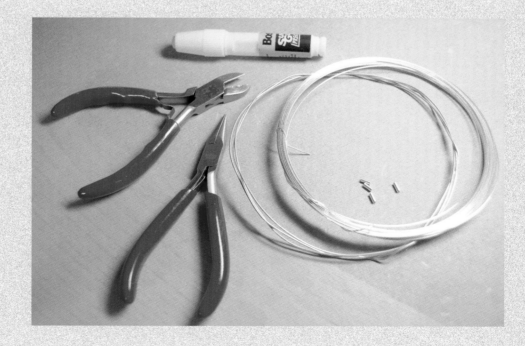

method

step 1 internal and external circle

a. Use formers such as a wooden mandrel, cup or cardboard tube, to create the internal circular core of 1 mm (0.04 in.) diameter wire. When formed, the circle should be roughly 60 mm (2.4 in.) in

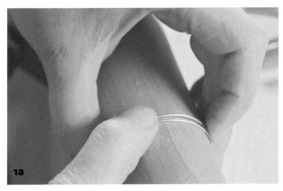

diameter, large enough to comfortably fit over your hand. Cut the circle to the correct length after forming, allowing for a 40 mm (1.5 in.) overlap.

b. Bind the ends with a small piece of masking tape, to help hold the form.

Repeat this process for the external circle, which should be roughly 90 mm (3.5 in.) in diameter, again allowing for an overlap.

step 2 begin to wrap wire

a. Hold the 0.7 mm (0.03 in.) wire against the outside core. Allow 35mm (1.4 in.) of the 0.7 mm (0.03 in.) wire to extend beyond, and using snipe-nosed pliers, bend it over the external core and wrap tightly 6 times.

b. **c**. Make sure there are no gaps between the coils. Pull the excess down towards the centre. DO NOT TRIM: You may need this extra length later to adjust the tension!

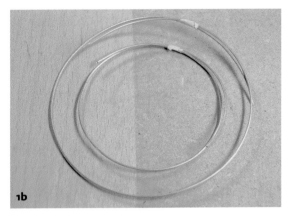

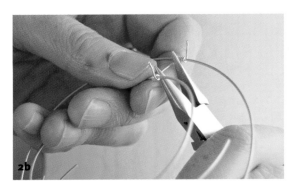

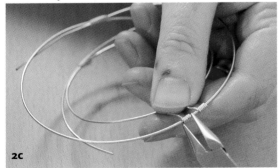

d. Position the internal core centrally inside the external core (there should be roughly 15 mm (0.6 in.) between them) and then hold the 0.7 wrapping wire across the gap between the circles. Cut the 0.7 wire allowing 20 mm (0.8 in.) to extend beyond the internal core. Now wrap as before, four times, and push the remaining end back towards the outside. DO NOT TRIM.

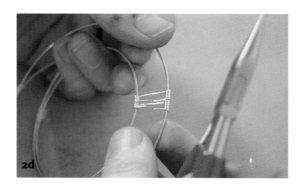

2d

e. Repeat this process, ensuring that each time the wrapping is on the same side of the wires. Add new wires in-between the radials you've already put in, this helps to ensure you keep the core wires parallel.

step 3 continue wrapping

Begin to spread out the radials around the circle. Remove the masking tape, as the radials will now hold the bracelet's form. These initial radials will help to maintain equidistance between the two core wires.

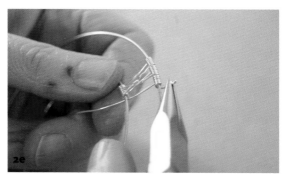

2e

Continue adding radials with the same amounts of wraps, until the circle is complete and you have overlapped by roughly 20 mm (0.8 in.) internally /30 mm (1.2 in.) externally. The last radial should be wrapped only twice around both core wires; when the crimps are in place the visual effect is better.

TIP

❝ You may find that your circles begin to pull together as you work; insert the tips of the pliers between the core wires and force them open to widen areas where the core wires are not parallel. ❞

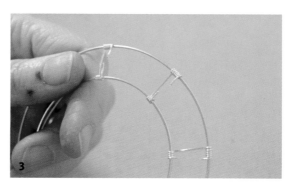

3

step 4 add crimps

Push the crimps onto the ends of the core wire, and force them against your radials to ensure good form. You may need to straighten the core wires to allow the crimps to move along.

Glue with superglue, and allow to dry.

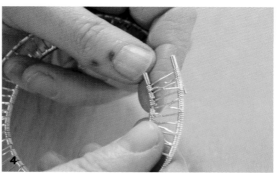

4

JEWELLERY USING TEXTILE TECHNIQUES

5a

5b

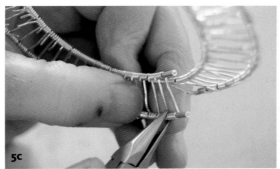

step 5 trim

Check the whole bracelet for tightness and regularity, both on the inner and outer circles.

a. Use the extra lengths of the radials to add extra coils if necessary, but be sure to intersperse evenly around the bracelet, otherwise the radials will look out of line.

b. Use side cutters to trim all the excess ends.

c. Use the snipe-nosed pliers to smooth the newly cut ends down and around the core.
You should find that they tuck neatly inside the gap made by the next radial along. File the crimped ends flush and smooth.

d. The bracelet is now ready to wear.

5c

5a

Vicky can be contacted by:
telephone: 0207 737 1524
e-mail: Vicky@sublime.net
www.vicky-forrester.com
Project photographs © Sarah Keay.

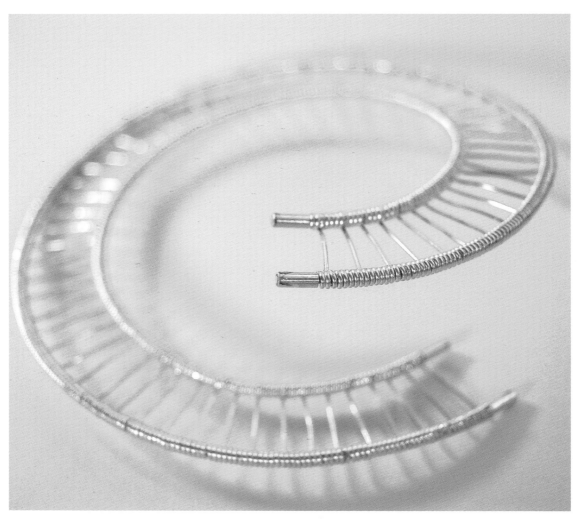

The finished bracelet.

gallery – vicky forrester

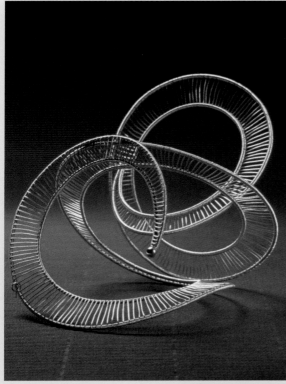

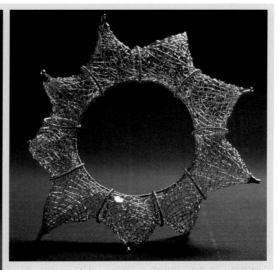

LEFT *Athene Arm*, 1999. Sterling silver. The technique for this piece is binding, however the framework is brought to a point at either end and then the silver is heated to a ball.

ABOVE *Spikey bangle*, 1999. Sterling silver. Basket weave which developed into a self-evolving form.

RIGHT *Venus neckpiece*, 1999. Plain weave using sterling silver wires. For *Venus neckpiece*, the wire form is initially constructed before thinner wires are woven into the open structure.

Photographs © S Bray.

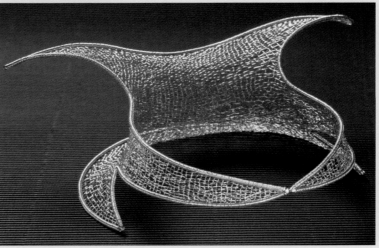

tanvi kant

"I use reclaimed textiles to make jewellery, such as old saris belonging to my family, unwanted furnishing fabrics or my own clothes, which I combine with hand-formed pieces of porcelain. My choice of materials refers to recycling and sustainability but they also give reference to more personal and collective histories.

The fabrics are transformed, and in some pieces their original form is visible, allowing the wearer to feel and remember the origins of the work. The methods of wearing by draping, wrapping and knotting also refer to the origins of the fabrics, such as the sari and scarf. The nature of materials and techniques used results in spontaneity within my making process, which reflects drawing-like qualities and diversity in colour, scale and texture.

My work has evolved from diverse sources and influences: the physical structure of the pieces being influenced by the study of plant cell structures and ethnographic tools, together with the association of adornment with cultural and religious rituals."

Tanvi Kant 2009

TOP LEFT *Two rings neckpiece*, 2006. Textile, porcelain.

TOP RIGHT *Looped rings neckpiece*, 2006. Textile, porcelain.

Photographs © Tanvi Kant.

ABOVE *Brown pink bracelet*, bracelet – stitched loops, 2008. Textile, porcelain.

LEFT *Brown pink necklace*, neckpiece – stitched loops, 2008. Textile, porcelain.

6 knitting

Knitting consists of loops called stitches that are pulled through one another. The active stitches are held on a needle until another loop can be passed through them. Knitting may be done by hand or by machine. Like weaving, knitting is a technique for producing a two-dimensional fabric from a one-dimensional yarn or thread. One of the earliest known examples of knitting was finely decorated cotton socks found in Egypt in the end of the first millennium AD.

By hand, there are numerous styles and methods. Flat knitting is done on two straight needles. It produces a flat length of fabric. Different yarns and knitting needles may be used to achieve different final outcomes, to give the final piece different colours, textures and weight. Circular knitting is done on circular or double-pointed needles and produces a seamless tube of fabric. In intarsia the yarns are used in well-segregated regions, e.g., a yellow sun on a blue sky. The yarns are kept on separate spools and only one is knitted at any time. Double knitting is more complicated than intarsia, whereby two or more yarns alternate repeatedly within one row and all the yarns must be carried along the row. This is most commonly seen in Fair Isle sweaters.

shetland rose lace tiara
by helen robertson

Shetland Lace is the name for the very fine and elaborate lace knitting produced in the Shetland Isles from the mid-nineteenth century onwards. At the height of its fashion status it was even presented to Royalty and shown at the Crystal Palace Exhibition in 1851. The most famous items of Shetland Lace were the wedding ring shawls. These were usually about six feet square and so finely knitted that they could be pulled through a wedding ring!

EQUIPMENT REQUIRED

- ▶ 2 x 3 mm (0.08 x 0.1 in.) knitting needles
- ▶ 1 pair of flat-nosed pliers
- ▶ 1 pair top cutters

MATERIALS REQUIRED

- ▶ 0.25 mm (0.009 in.) or 0.2 mm (0.008 in.) fine silver wire
- ▶ freshwater baroque pearls 5–6 mm (0.2–0.23 in.) or beads of your own choice
- ▶ silver-plated tiara band

Helen can be contacted by:
telephone: 01806 522619
e-mail: helen@lunnister.plus.com
www.helenrobertson.co.uk
Project photographs © Andrew Inkster.

JEWELLERY USING TEXTILE TECHNIQUES

method

step 1 cast on
Cast on 13 stitches leaving a long tail of approx.
1 metre (3.3 ft) of silver wire.

step 2 wind wire
Wind up the long tail of wire
into a coil to prevent it from
getting in the way.

step 3 start to knit
Start knitting following the pattern.

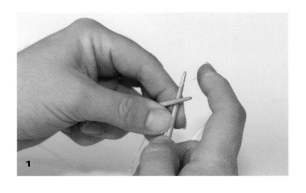

TIP

❝ To avoid breaking the wire only uncoil
small lengths at a time and straighten
any kinks that occur. ❞

		O	X	O						
	O	X	O	\	O					
\	O				O	/				
	\	O		O	/					

KEY \ and / = two stitches
together
O = make one

X = slip one, knit two together,
pass slipped stitch over
blanks = knit

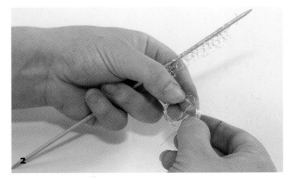

step 4 pull
Pull down gently on the knitting after every few
rows to keep it in shape.

step 5 continue

Continue knitting the pattern.

step 6 complete motifs

Continue knitting until all of the 7 motifs have been completed (i.e. repeat pattern seven times).

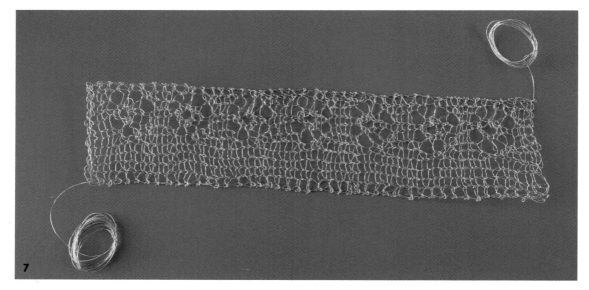

step 7 cast off

Cast off leaving a long end of about 1 m (3.3 ft), wind up this end as before into a coil.

step 8 attach

Attach the knitting to the tiara band. Start by gently bending the first row of the tiara around the tiara band.

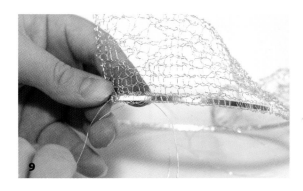

step 9 sew in place

Gently unfurl the wound up ends of wire and use them to sew the knitted piece onto the tiara band.

step 10 add pearls

Make sure that the knitted piece is centred onto the tiara band. Once in place sew on the pearls.

step 11 snip

Pull the ends through a pearl with the pliers and snip using the top cutters.

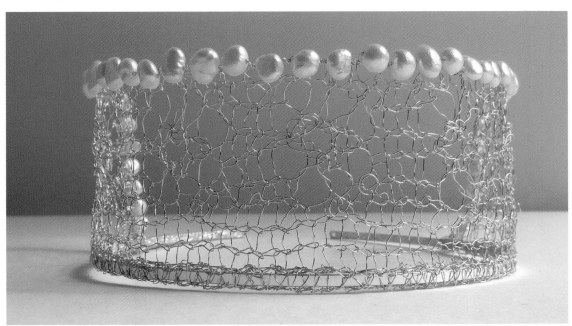

The finished tiara. Photograph © Helen Robertson.

Julie's necklace by Helen Robertson, 2001. Pearls, fine silver and Swarovski crystals.
Photograph © Helen Robertson.

gallery – lisa juen

"The world around us changes, mixes, grows, becomes a melting pot of different people and cultures. This development offers a lot of advantages in terms of communication and exchange. Globalisation helps us to unite the world, but also threatens to homogenise difference and individuality.

'Higher, faster, better' seems to be the idea that is settled in the human mind, being influenced by advertisement and stimulus satiation. The outside world becomes more and more important and in turn the internal world, developing one's own uninfluenced ideas, seems to loose its value. For the individual to find a way to break out of that dynamic becomes more and more difficult. In a time of satellite systems, mobile phones, identity cards and CCTV surveillance, a physical escape is doomed to remain a dream. While the adventurers of ancient times could look at the horizon and imagine, dreaming today is interfered with by skyscrapers and television broadcasts.

One way of escape I think, can be found in a self-created realm of fantasy; there one might find a way to feel free, to indulge one's needs and desires."

"My work is concerned with the idea of finding access to the world of dreams, desires and wishes. I view my pieces as witnesses of experiences made in reality, but being transferred to a place of fantasy. The pieces are meant to offer the viewer access points, pathways and doors to the world of dreaming and the inner self.

There we find the resources and strength needed to carry on living in reality.

Without dreams, one becomes a robot." Lisa Juen 2009

ABOVE *Snembryo*, brooch, 2007. Enamel on steel, silk floss, stainless steel pins.

LEFT *Learning to Let Go*, brooch, 2007. Enamel on steel, silk floss, ink on paper, stainless steel pin.

Photographs © Lisa Juen.

gallery – andrée wejsmann

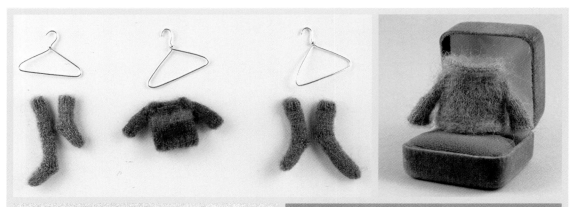

CLOCKWISE FROM ABOVE

Sticks and Stones, is part of a series of framed works, but can also be worn as a brooch. 2005.

Finger Sweater is a ring (also part of a series). It is hand-knit mohair, approx. 2 cm (0.8 in.) high. 2004.

Sweater Chair is part of a set of two sterling silver watch fobs; the set is called, *You can't catch a cold like that*. They measure approximately 4 cm (1.5 in.) high, and are all fabricated by hand. 2004.

Too Long Sleeve, is part of a series of framed works, but can also be worn as a brooch. 2005.

Photographs © Andrée Wejsmann.

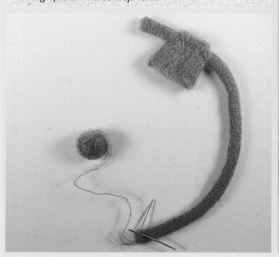

claire lowe

"My work is influenced by form, texture and colour, and is very much about exploration and combination of materials including mixed media, metal and plastics (mainly resin).

Contradictory textures and feelings are seen in the knitted/woollen range, putting soft surfaces and materials inside hard plastic and creating a visual texture without a sensory feeling.

I produce small batch productions of contemporary jewellery, which sell through shops and art galleries around the country as well as making specific conceptual pieces for exhibitions."

Claire Lowe, 2009.

Photographs © Claire Lowe.

ABOVE *Bangle*, 2007. Polyester resin, knitted wool, button.

BELOW *Bangle*, 2007. Polyester resin, knitted wool, button.

7 french knitting

French knitting, spool knitting, or corking is a form of knitting that uses a spool or bobbin, with usually four nails hammered in place, to produce a narrow tube of knitting. French knitting is the traditional method to teach children the basic principles of knitting.

how to french knit a wire bangle

EQUIPMENT REQUIRED

▸ 1 wooden bobbin, (either 4, 6 or 8 pegged)
▸ 1 crochet hook
▸ scissors
▸ round-nose pliers

MATERIAL REQUIRED

▸ 1 reel 0.5 mm (0.02 in.) wire

method

step 1 winding on

Holding the bobbin firmly with the thumb in front, push the end of the wire down through the centre of the bobbin, leaving about 7.5 cm (3 in.) spare. In a clockwise direction, wind the wire around each peg, wrapping from right to left.

TIP

❝ Remember not to pull the wire too tight when knitting your first round! ❞

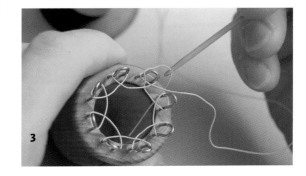

3

step 2 two on one peg

Once you have wound the wire around all of the pegs, place the wire around the front of the first peg so that you have 2 loops on the one peg.

step 3 pull one over

Using the crochet hook, pull the lower loop over the top of the peg. Carry on this process for each peg in turn, continuing in a clockwise direction.

step 4 carry on

Carry on knitting as before until the necklace has reached the desired length.

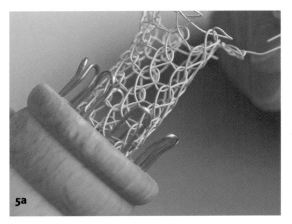

5a

step 5 casting off

a. To finish knitting the first chain link, unhook all of the loops from the bobbin. Cut the wire using the scissors, leaving plenty of wire to work with. Loop this extra wire once through the last loop to prevent it unravelling.

Gently stretch the tube of knitting so that it is an even width all the way along.

b. To join the ends continue to loop the wire through each opposite loop until the ends have joined completely.

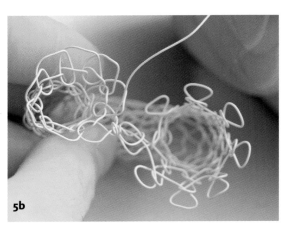

5b

c. Continue this process until you have the desired length of chain, by looping each new link into the one before. For the bangle pictured I knitted 10 links, however you can include as many as you wish.

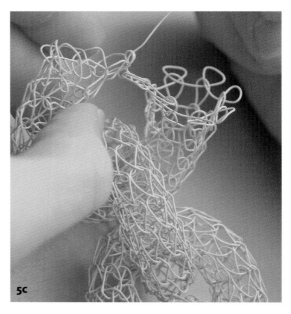

5c

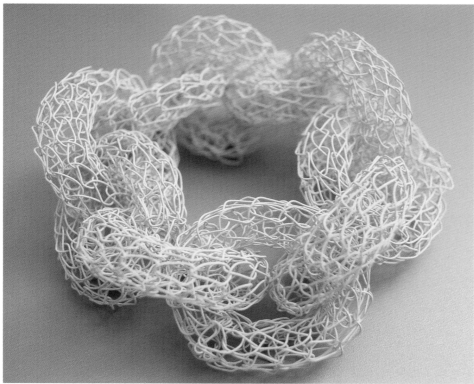

The finished bangle.

JEWELLERY USING TEXTILE TECHNIQUES

8 weaving

Weaving consists of interlacing at right angles two or more series of flexible materials (in our case silver wire), of which the longitudinal are called warp and the transverse weft.

silver wire bracelet handmade on manual loom by lilia breyter

EQUIPMENT REQUIRED

- fine silver wire 0.2/0.3 mm (22/20 gauge) diameter
- sterling silver wire 0.4 mm (18 gauge) diameter
- findings
- epoxy adhesive
- cotton thread

MATERIALS REQUIRED

- loom
- shuttle
- pliers
- snips
- press

For my work I use different fabric structures, such as plain cloth, twill and gauze.

In plain cloth, warp and weft pass over and under each other alternately. Twill forms diagonal ribs in fabrics and these are due to the intervals at which warp and weft are intersected. Thus, two or more warp threads (silver wire) are passed over or under one or more than one weft thread (silver wire) in regular succession. Twills can be woven in different angles, zigzag, squares and other geometrical designs.

In crossed weaving (gauze) warp threads (silver wire) intertwine amongst themselves to give intermediate effects between ordinary weaving and lace. All these patterns can be used in different combinations to create all the designs you can imagine. With the thickness of wire used by me only the weft is seen, except in gauze.

I use a small manual loom. It has front and back rods moved by
ratchets. Sticks are attached to the rods and a three positions rigid
heddle shaft. The warp threads pass alternately through a heddle
and through a space between the heddles, so that raising the shaft
will raise half the threads (those passing through the heddles), and
lowering the shaft will lower the same threads – the threads passing
through the spaces between the heddles remain in place. The rigid
heddle I use has 7 threads per cm (15 threads per inch).

Any manual loom can be used.

method

step 1 warping

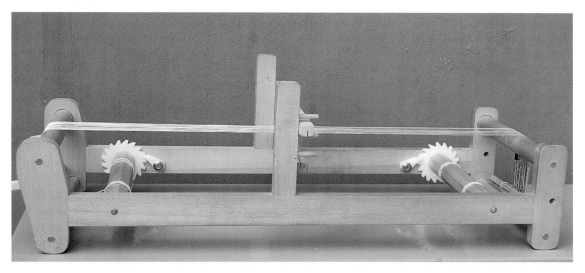

Loom with warp.

Use sterling silver wire 0.4 mm (18 gauge) diameter.

To set up the warp (width) you must measure the desired width in the rigid heddle; because there is no shrinkage, all warp threads remain parallel. With my rigid heddle I need 12 pairs of warp threads to weave a 46 mm (1.8 in.) wide bracelet.

I cut strands of the necessary length to weave the bracelet. To calculate the length of each one we must add about 25 cm (9 in.) of loom waste. I usually prepare my loom for weaving three bracelets. So, if we add three 18 cm (7 in.) long bracelets, plus the separation between them of about 1.2 cm (0.5 in.) and additional waste length, each pair must be about 77–80 cm (30–32 in.).

Thirteen strands of 1.60 m (63 in.) are necessary (twelve plus one more because the warp edges are best double for greater strength).

I pass the wire through the holes of the stick attached to the back rod. Each thread is two ply, after doing that I pass each one through the

Heddles and warp.

heddles and tie them to the front rod stick with pliers. The same must be done with all the threads. Remember that the two outside threads must be double. (This method will vary depending on the type of loom used) **but all of this process must be done very carefully in order to maintain equal tension in the entire warp**.

step 2 weaving

The fine silver wire 0.27–0.30 mm (22–20 gauge) diameter must be stored on the shuttle.

TIP

" Do all the work slowly and carefully. Wire is much less forgiving than yarn. It will kink easily, it can also break if it is reworked too much. "

1	2	3	4	5	6	7	8	9	10	11	12	

Repeat 5 times these 2 rows

Repeat 5 times these 2 rows

Repeat 5 times these 2 rows

Repeat 5 times these 2 rows

Repeat 5 times these 2 rows

Repeat 5 times these 2 rows

Repeat 5 times these 2 rows

Repeat 5 times these 2 rows

The shuttle is a tool designed to neatly and compactly hold the weft yarn while weaving. Shuttles are thrown or passed back and forth through the shed between the yarn threads of the warp in order to weave in the weft. I use the simplest shuttles, known as 'stick shuttles' made from a flat, narrow piece of wood with notches on the ends to hold the weft yarn. I start by weaving eight or ten rows of plain weave with cotton thread to prevent the wire fabric from slipping. Then I begin weaving with silver wire 0.8 cm (0.3 in.) plain cloth and 16.5 cm (6.5 in.) of the selected pattern finishing the bracelet with another 0.8 cm (0.3 in.) weaving plain cloth. The pattern of this bracelet is twill 3/1 zigzag. For weaving it follow the diagram shown top right.

TIP

" Consider this pattern as only one of the multiple possibilities that you can create as you increase your skill with the loom and metal wire. "

Vertical lines of squares represent warp threads, horizontal lines represent weft threads. A dark square indicates that the warp thread it represents is above the weft, whereas a blank means weft above warp. Repeat this pattern until the desired length is reached. At the end of the first bracelet,

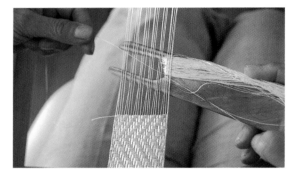

Weaving right.

Weaving left.

I weave 1.2 cm (0.5 in.) with cotton thread. Then I weave the second and third bracelets that could be of other patterns and lengths but will be the same width.

step 3 finishing

When the bracelet/bracelets are completed, take off the wire fabric from the loom, and separate one piece from another by cutting the silver threads, leaving 8 mm (0.3 in.) each ending thread length.

a. **b**. Then ply those ending wires 180° and press them over the piece.

c. To make this work wearable you need a catch. There are many different sorts of findings that can be used. You can either fabricate one yourself or purchase it from companies who stock commercial findings.

TIP

66 The list of suppliers in the appendix may be of some help to you in sourcing such components. 99

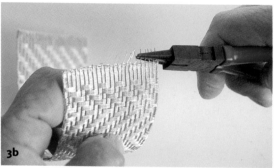

I use cold connections because the temperature required for soldering is too high for the silver wire.

The finding can be connected by an adhesive or by riveting it in place. In this case I have used epoxy. You must use one that bonds quickly and will stay strong and colourless for as long as possible.

d. Press the buckle of the piece during the full time recommended by the epoxy manufacturer.

By varying the weaving width and length, it is possible to make bracelets, chokers, pendants, earrings, and whatever your imagination suggests.

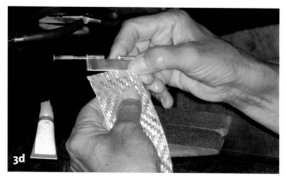

The finished bangle.

Lilia can be contacted by:
telephone: (54)(11) 4742 3014
e-mail: info@platatextil.com.ar
Project photographs © Paula Breyter.

gallery – lilia breyter

JEWELLERY USING TEXTILE TECHNIQUES

Lilia recently obtained a Certificate of Excellence in Handicraft for her silver wire loom weaving by UNESCO (United Nations Educational, Scientific and Cultural Organization) for Argentina.

Twill zig zag bracelet, 2007. Sterling silver and fine silver.

Photograph © Paula Breyter.

willemijn de greef

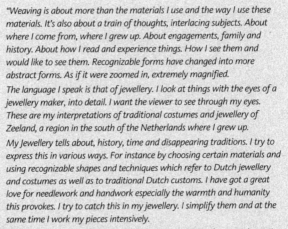

"Weaving is about more than the materials I use and the way I use these materials. It's also about a train of thoughts, interlacing subjects. About where I come from, where I grew up. About engagements, family and history. About how I read and experience things. How I see them and would like to see them. Recognizable forms have changed into more abstract forms. As if it were zoomed in, extremely magnified.

The language I speak is that of jewellery. I look at things with the eyes of a jewellery maker, into detail. I want the viewer to see through my eyes. These are my interpretations of traditional costumes and jewellery of Zeeland, a region in the south of the Netherlands where I grew up.

My Jewellery tells about, history, time and disappearing traditions. I try to express this in various ways. For instance by choosing certain materials and using recognizable shapes and techniques which refer to Dutch jewellery and costumes as well as to traditional Dutch customs. I have got a great love for needlework and handwork especially the warmth and humanity this provokes. I try to catch this in my jewellery. I simplify them and at the same time I work my pieces intensively.

I search for sketchy images which often don't avoid roughness and question the concept of beauty. I play with the weight and the size of the pieces. I explore the borders of wearability. Due to their size the pieces sometimes refer to ethnic jewellery as well as to traditional professions like fishery."
Willemijn de Greef, 2008.

TOP LEFT *Necklace: Halssieraad Rood*, 2006. Wool, imitation coral, thread, plastic. 140 x 50 x 5 cm (55 x 19.5 x 2 in.).

LEFT *Necklace: Halsieraad Wit*, 2006. Cotton, rope. 95 x 35 x 9 cm (37 x 14 x 3.5 in.).

BELOW *Necklace: Halssieraad Mosterd*, 2005. Zinc, teakwood, cotton. 30 cm (12 in.).

Photographs © Willemijn de Greef.

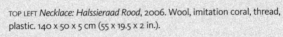

kathleen bailey

"The hand-woven threads I created for the amulets in the castaway collection are a colourful, yet subtle solution that complements their delicacy. Recently I have amalgamated elements from previous collections, such as the haphazard enamelling and the simple horseshoes of the relic work. The textile threads and embroidery are prominent building blocks holding the work together both physically and aesthetically." Kathleen Bailey 2009

Photographs © Kathleen Bailey.

ABOVE *Castaway pendant*, 2008. 18ct gold, driftwood, shells, glass found on the beach, carved acrylic catches, hand-woven threads in cotton.

LEFT *Handwoven threads*, 2008. Cotton.

RIGHT *Castaway earrings*, 2008. 18ct gold, driftwood, shells, glass found on the beach, carved acrylic catches, hand-woven threads in cotton.

9 bobbin lace

Bobbin lace, as the name suggests, is made with bobbins and a pillow. The bobbins, traditionally turned from wood, bone or plastic, hold threads which are woven together and held in place with pins that are stuck in the pattern on the pillow. The pillow contains straw or other materials such as sawdust, insulation styrofoam or ethafoam to give a firm base to work on.

wire lace flower pendant by sarah smith

This design can be made using cotton, embroidery thread or whatever else you wish.

EQUIPMENT REQUIRED

- ▸ approximately 100 pins with heads
- ▸ a cork with a needle inserted into it, sharp end facing out
- ▸ 8 clothes pegs consisting of 4 different colours. In the photos I have used 2 pink pegs, 2 white pegs, 2 natural wood pegs and 2 green pegs
- ▸ a permanent marker to label the pegs
- ▸ pencil
- ▸ scissors
- ▸ pliers
- ▸ needle

MATERIALS REQUIRED

- ▸ 1 x 10 m (33 ft) reel of 0.2 mm (0.008 in.) round silver wire
- ▸ a piece of stiff card 12 cm by 8 cm (4.5 x 3 in.)
- ▸ a square piece of polystyrene at least 30 cm by 30 cm (12 x 12 in.) covered with fabric (you can just pin the fabric in place)
- ▸ tracing paper
- ▸ coloured beads that will allow 0.2 mm (0.008 in.) wire to pass through them (in the flower pendant I have used 5 but you could add more)
- ▸ a jump link large enough to allow your necklace to pass through
- ▸ a necklace (a piece of ribbon could be used if you don't have a necklace)

method

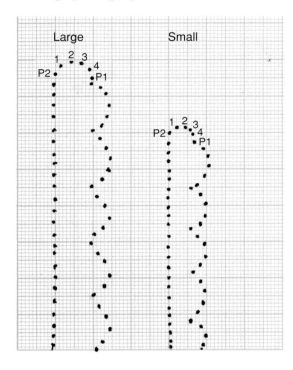

Large   Small

step 1 – pattern

Trace the pattern onto the tracing paper. Then pin this over the card.

Using the cork with the needle embedded into it, prick the pattern onto the card. Once you have pricked the whole pattern remove and discard the tracing paper.

Pin the card onto the polystyrene cushion using 4 pins, one in each corner. Put 4 pins into the first 4 top holes, noted by 1, 2, 3, 4, on the pattern.

step 2 – cut wire

Measure and cut 1m (39 in.) of silver wire. Hold the two cut ends to find the middle of the length then make a little fold in the wire. Now coil up each side of the wire to stop them from getting in the way, coiling up to about 10 cm (4 in.) from the centre fold.

Place a clothes peg on the end of each coil (make sure that you put two clothes pegs of the same colour on both coils). Now mark the two pegs with a W1 and W2.

These pegs are your workers and will be moving to and fro across the wire lace. In the example piece these pegs are pink and marked with W1 and W2.

Now measure 50 cm (19.5 in.) of the silver wire and again find the mid-point of the wire and mark this with a fold. Coil the wire each side until it is 10 cm (4 in.) from the fold then peg the coils with 2 pegs of the same colour. Mark these pegs 3 and 4. These pegs are called the passive pegs (pegs 3 and 4 are green in the example).

Repeat this step twice again, labelling the pegs, 5, 6, 7 and 8 (pegs 5 and 6 being natural wood and 7 and 8 being white in the worked example).

step 3 – place on pattern
- Place the pink worker pegs 1 and 2 over pin 1.
- Place the green passive pegs 3 and 4 over pin 2.
- Place the natural wood passive pegs 5 and 6 over pin 3.
- Place the white passive pegs 7 and 8 over pin 4.

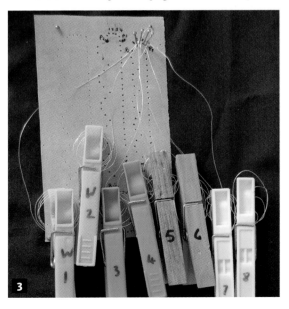

Now you are ready to start learning the basic lace making technique called the cloth stitch.

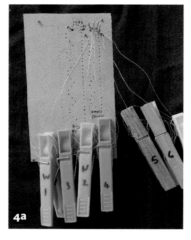

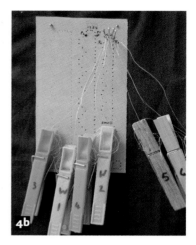

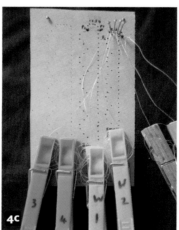

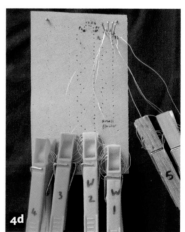

step 4 how to do the cloth stitch

a. Start with the pink peg worker pair W1 and W2. These are going to do a stitch with the green pegs 3 and 4. Cross pink worker peg 2 over green passive peg 3. Your peg sequence should now read 1, 3, 2, 4.

b. Next pick up green pegs 3 and 4, peg 3 being in the left hand and peg 4 being in the right. Move them so that the green peg 3 is now in front of the pink peg 1 and green peg 4 is in front of pink peg 2. Your peg sequence should now read 3, 1, 4, 2.

c. The next move in the stitch is to switch pink peg 1 over green peg 4 so that both pink worker pegs 1 and 2 are side by side and ready to move on to do a cloth stitch with the next pair. Your peg sequence should now read 3, 4, 1, 2.

d. Lastly pick up green peg 4 in your left hand and pink peg 2 in your right and lift them over the other 2 pegs so that your sequence reads 4, 3, 2, 1.

step 5 repeat stitch

Repeat a cloth stitch with the pink worker pair and the natural wood pair.

Before the first move the sequence should read 2, 1, 5, 6.

- The first move being 2, 5, 1, 6
- The second being 5, 2, 6, 1
- The third being 5, 6, 2, 1
- The fourth being 6, 5, 1, 2

The pink worker pair should again be side by side to do a cloth stitch with white pair 7 and 8.

step 6 repeat stitch again

Repeat a cloth stitch with the pink worker pair and the white pair.

Before the first move the peg sequence being 1, 2, 7, 8.

- The peg sequence for the first move being 1, 7, 2, 8
- The second being 7, 1, 8, 2
- The third being 7, 8, 1, 2
- The fourth being 8, 7, 2, 1

You are now ready to place your first pin in.

The pin goes into P1. Holding both pink worker pegs in your right hand and a pin in your left put the pin in so that the wire on both the pink pegs goes around the pin and hangs down ready to work back across to the next pin hole on the left.

Carefully tighten all the wires, pulling the wire above the pegs to tighten up the stitches. Tighten each stitch individually.

Remember not to pull the pegs to tighten the stitches as the wire coil will just slip out of the peg!

Hold all the passive pairs by placing your hand across the pegs and gently pulling each worker pair one at a time. This should tighten up the wire lace.

step 7 work back across

Now you are ready to work back across to the next pin hole on the left.

Repeat a cloth stitch with the pink worker pair and the white pair.

Before the first move the sequence should be 8, 7, 2, 1.

- The peg sequence for the first move being 8, 2, 7, 1
- The second being 2, 8, 1, 7
- The third being 2, 1, 8, 7
- The fourth being 1, 2, 7, 8

Now do a cloth stitch again to the left with the pink worker pair and the natural wood pair.

Before the first move the sequence should be 6, 5, 1, 2.

- The peg sequence being 6, 1, 5, 2
- The second being 1, 6, 2, 5
- The third being 1, 2, 6, 5
- The fourth being 2, 1, 5, 6

To complete the row now cloth stitch the pink worker pair to the green passive pair.

Before the first move the sequence should be 4, 3, 2, 1.

- The peg sequence for the first move being 4, 2, 3, 1
- The second being 2, 4, 1, 3
- The third being 2, 1, 4, 3
- The fourth being 1, 2, 3, 4

Now holding the pink worker pair in the left hand and a pin in the right insert the pin so that the wires on the worker pair hang down round the pin and ready to work back across to the right. Repeat tightening up the stitch as described above.

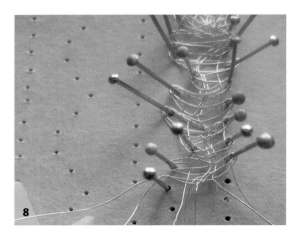

step 8 repeat stitch

Repeat the sequencing steps above, working the pink worker pair from left to right and back again, ensuring that you place a pin at the end of each row in the hole that you previously pricked.

Continue until all the pricked holes on the pattern have a pin in place.

TIP

⁶⁶ It is very important that you follow the stitch pattern exactly! ⁹⁹

step 9 tie off

Once you have placed the last pin in the last hole you are now ready to tie off the pairs.

Pick up the pink worker pairs and tie them in a knot left over right.

Then tie the pink pairs again in a knot right over left. Repeat this process with the other 3 pairs. Once all the pairs have been tied you can cut the wire.

You can now remove the pins and take the wire lace from the card.

TIP

⁶⁶ When cutting the wire leave enough to sew into the lace so that there are no jagged ends. ⁹⁹

step 10 sewing up the flower

a. Sew up one side of the flower, concentrating on a few stitches at a time Gently pull on the wire. The wire lace should start to curve, eventually forming a circle once the whole length of one side has been sewn. Tuck in any ends so there are no jagged bits.

b. Now sew up the two ends so that the flower is complete; again tucking in any ends.

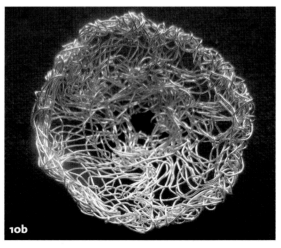

step 11 making the larger flower

Repeat the process as for the first flower using the large flower tracing.

step 12 making the stamens

Cut about 10 cm (4 in.) of wire and place a bead onto it. Slide the bead to the mid-point of the wire then twist the wire to hold the bead in place. Repeat this process again to get the desired number of stamens.

Thread the stamens through the lace of the inner flower and using the silver wire sew the stamens in the desired place on the inner flower. Tuck in the ends.

step 13 putting it all together

Attach the smaller flower to the larger flower with a couple of stitches ensuring that all ends are tucked into the inner of the flower.

step 14 finish

Sew a jump link to the back of the outer flower so that a necklace can be attached. Make sure that the jump link is large enough to allow the necklace to be threaded through.

Your pendant is now ready to wear!

Sarah can be contacted by:
telephone: 07933 755019
e-mail: sarahlouisefleming@yahoo.co.uk
Project photographs © Sarah Smith.

The finished pendant.

10 sewing

stille by sarah kettley

'*Stille*' *is a neckpiece which explores the boundary between intimate space and public performance. It attempts to capture that moment when we gather ourselves, perhaps find some kind of inner space, before a performative event. Colours and patterns have been inspired by a first visit to Australia, drawing on the Owl Eye Moth, gum tree barks and grasses, while the concept itself began with the flight of a Rosella overhead, and that momentary flash of brilliant colour. The sounds were collected over the course of the project, new sounds to this visitor from Scotland, like the birds calling first thing in the morning; and the many sounds of water, from the drainpipes on the single day of rain we've had in the last three weeks, to the surf and cicadas of Kaiola. These have in turn inspired the sounds that are available to the wearer as they roll their head to the front and sides; we are so used to the notion of surround sound as something large scale and imposing – here in contrast it is an intimate event.*

Sarah Kettley 2007

The collar is screen-printed with conductive silver ink and incorporates 'soft' electronics using conductive yarns. The project demonstrates the use of conductive textiles in digital or interactive designs. The pigment in the silver ink is at a high enough density to be conductive, and is used in the neckline of the collar to create open switches, which are closed by skin contact when the wearer either grabs and strokes them, or when they roll their head across the patches: three separate switches play three small sounds through speakers mounted in the collar.

The collar was developed in 2007 at reSkin, an intensive wearables media lab run by ANAT, the Australian Network for the Arts and Technology in conjunction with Craft Australia.

EQUIPMENT REQUIRED

- *Arduino* microprocessor controller
- 9v battery
- electronic components:
  resistors
  breadboarding kit
  multimeter
- 3 small speakers

MATERIALS REQUIRED

- conductive thread
- conductive velcro
- conductive silver epoxy
- conductive silver ink
- interfacing
- sewing thread and needle
- iron-on lightweight interfacing
- heavy (stiff) interfacing
- a range of fabric scraps (cotton, polyester etc.)

method

step 1 template

Draw out the template and cut out the pattern in fabric on a tailor's dummy.

step 2 screen-print

Screen-print the conductive silver ink.

TIP

❝ Placing pairs of motifs on the collar allows for a number of switches. ❞

step 3 attach interfacing

Stitch or bondaweb the heavy interfacing onto the back collar.

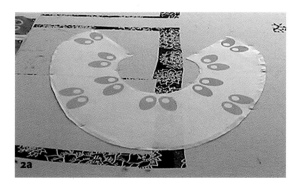

2a

2b

4a

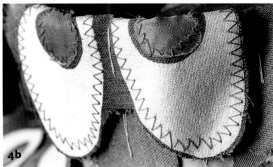

4b

step 4 stitch fabric

Stitch the fabric scraps to the front collar.

step 5 design circuit

Design the circuit according to resistance of the conductive yarns and printed switches. Model it on the breadboard with wires and the speakers. In this design the three speakers are placed one under each ear and one under the chin.

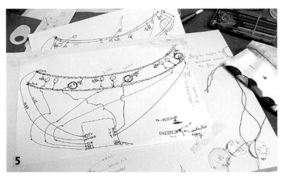

5

step 6 test

Test conductive threads for conductivity and resistance using a multimeter.

step 7 attach circuit

Stitch the circuit design using the conductive threads, using the iron-on lightweight webbing as insulation. Finish joins between the soft textile and any hard components using the conductive silver epoxy.

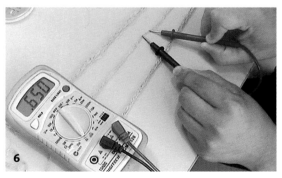

6

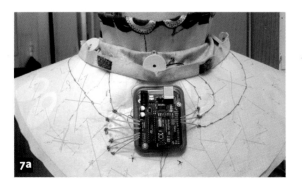

7a

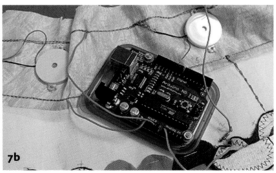

7b

step 8 programme Arduino

Programme the Arduino processor using the Arduino programming environment. This is where you set the conditions (input) that trigger the sounds (output).

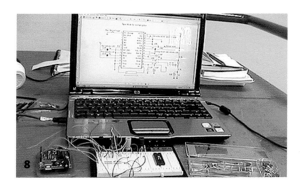

```
* turns on and off a light emitting diode(LED) connected to digital
* pin 13. The amount of time the LED will be on and off depends on
* the value obtained by analogRead(). In the easiest case we connect
* a potentiometer to analog pin 2.
*
* Created 1 December 2005
* copyleft 2005 DojoDave <http://www.0j0.org>
* http://arduino.berlios.de
*/

int inPin = 0;    // select the input pin for the potentiometer
int ledPin = 13;  // select the pin for the LED
int val = 0;      // variable to store the value coming from the sensor

void setup() {
  pinMode(13, OUTPUT); // declare the ledPin as an OUTPUT

void loop() {
  val = analogRead(inPin);  // read the value from the sensor
  digitalWrite(13, HIGH);   // turn the ledPin on
  delay(val);               // stop the program for some time
  digitalWrite(13, LOW);    // turn the ledPin off
  delay(val);               // stop the program for some time
```

step 9 sounds

Code the sounds still using the breadboarded circuit and the Arduino programming environment. (The code shown is an example only, not the actual one used.) The sounds in Stille are of crickets and frogs – creatures that come out in the rain, and were developed with the help of Stephen Barass, CSIRO Canberra.

step 10 finish

Sew the collar together. The collar is now complete.

Sarah can be contacted by:
telephone: 07980 609515
e-mail: works@sarahkettley.com
www.sarahkettley.com
Project photographs © Sarah Kettley.
Final Photograph © Mile Byrne, Faction Photography and the artist.

The finished collar.

gallery – sarah kettley

One of eight networked pieces in a sound and jewellery installation, using Speckled Computing prototype technology and a wide range of mixed materials. The pieces in ensemble were made to be played with; movement and touch altered the sound playing in the space.

Rope, 2006/2007. Cast resin, Speckled Computer prototype (custom electronics), French knitting with cotton and wire.

LEFT *Rope* (*detail*). The French knitting in *Rope* used a large arrangement of bobbins to give different scales and formal properties to the rope. The final piece is in actual fact made up of four separate pieces of knitting. One of them incorporates a plastic-coated wire, which connects to the micro-processor, and acts as a sensor.

Photographs © Mike Byrne, Faction Photography.

JEWELLERY USING TEXTILE TECHNIQUES

lucy sarneel

"A piece of jewellery invites to contemplate and evokes thoughts and emotions.

The basic idea for my pieces of jewellery derives from daily life experiences, thoughts and wonder in which the notion of time plays an important role. We all try to deal with personal lifetime, historic time and universal time.

Nature is an important point of reference; the question about the naturalness or artificiality of nature fascinates me and results in forms that remind us of flowers, plants or twigs.

Also antique textiles (of traditional costumes of little villages near Amsterdam) occur in my work, referring to disappearing costume traditions." Lucy Sarneel, 2009

RIGHT *Necklace Sentier du jardin*, 2007. Zinc, antique textile on rubber, nylon thread. Diameter 32 cm (12.5 in.).

BELOW *Necklace Fleurs de style II*, 2008. Zinc, antique textile on rubber, nylon thread. Diameter 25 cm (10 in.).

BELOW RIGHT *Brooch*, 2007. Zinc, sewing thread, silver (pin), nylon thread. 10.5 cm length x 13 cm width x 1 cm height (4 x 5 x 0.4 in.).

Photographs © Lucy Sarneel.

lina peterson

"The main focus of my work lies within the exploration of material qualities and combinations. I often use traditional 'craft' techniques, such as wood-carving and embroidery, but always used with a certain deliberate naivety. Drawing each piece together is the use of colour, which is often strong and playful.

The use of textiles in my work comes from my interest in how, when we wear a piece of jewellery, it forms a relationship with the garments that we wear. Be it a brooch that is pinned to a lapel or a necklace falling over a dress, the piece will change depending on what we wear. Using fabric and techniques inspired by textiles in my work makes this relationship even more tangible."
Lina Peterson, 2009.

LEFT *Stitched brooch*, 2007. Stitched textiles, plastic dip-coated back.

BELOW *Embroidered brooch*, 2006. Electroformed gold-plated copper, embroidered textile.

Photographs © Lina Peterson.

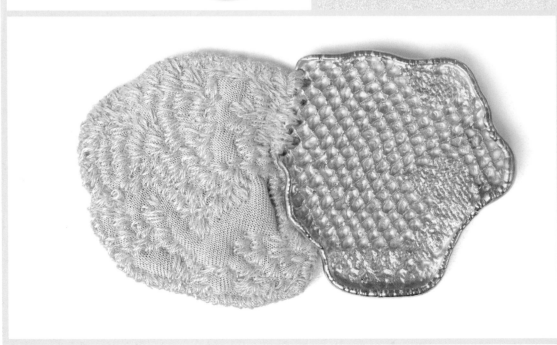

louise billgren

"The purpose of my jewellery is to tell a story in collaboration with the body. The stories often revolve around a woman's universe. Truly fascinated and also a little bit repulsed by this universe, I attempt to find ways to express myself artistically through forms and materials that are almost too feminine, too soft, too pink, too much and combine these with my love and affection for traditional craftsmanship."
Louise Billgren, 2009.

Wet kisses, from the Full Treatment Collection. Terrycloth, silver, mother of pearl, thread and silicone.

Wet Kisses plays with the notion of a more practical side to escapism and luxury in everyday life and materials.

Photograph © Axel Ryding.

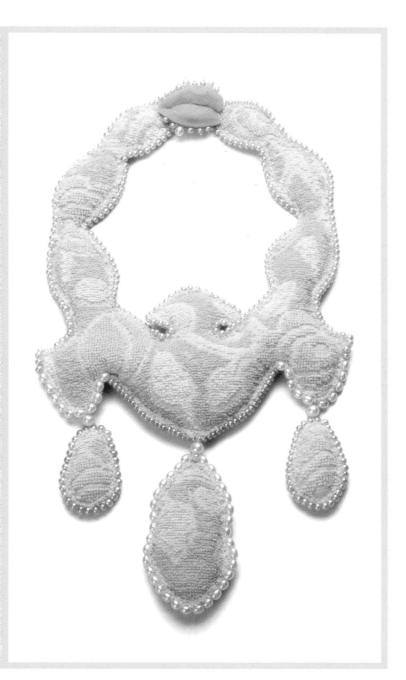

myung urso

"My contemporary jewellery aesthetic engages sculptural and painterly approaches towards creating art and in doing so the integrity of the form and its surface play a vital role in shaping my jewellery designs.

Oriental calligraphy and traditional embroidery, which I have practiced since I was young, has always fascinated me.

Colourful silk fabric, raw silk and cotton fabric are stretched and sewn over sculptural sterling silver wire forms. Their surfaces are often enriched with black ink brush strokes and hand stitching.

Applied lacquer on the fabric surfaces enhances the beauty, tension and durability of my jewellery forms."

Myung Urso, 2008.

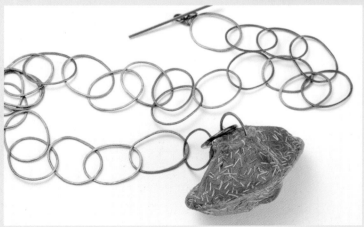

TOP *Neckpiece, Infinity*, 2008. Silk, thread, sterling silver. 24 x 40 x 0.5 cm (9.5 x 15.5 x 0.2 in.). Detail top left.

ABOVE *Harvest*, 2008. Silk, oriental ink, thread, sterling silver, lacquer. 21.5(h) x 21.5(w) x 2(d) cm (8.5 x 8.5 x 0.8 in.).

LEFT *Drop*, 2008. Silk, thread, sterling silver. 90(h) x 3.5(w) x 5.5(d) cm (35.5 x 3.5 x 2.2 in.).

Photographs © Timothy J. Fuss.

11 hand spinning

I n these pieces the old newspaper has been recycled and hand spun into a yarn. The only colour in the piece derives from the paper and print alone.

handspun paper
by sarah keay

EQUIPMENT REQUIRED

▶ scissors
▶ spool: or old wire reel

MATERIALS REQUIRED

▶ old newspapers

Paper in general can be woven for use into a huge variety of designs, from intricate pieces of jewellery to large rugs and beyond.

how to make your own handspun paper

Here's a quick fire way to get you started with the process:

method

step 1 fold paper
Take a page from an old newspaper and fold it into four.

step 2 cut strips
With the scissors cut 1 cm (0.4 in.) strips along the width.

step 3 twist
Start by twisting a strip tightly between your fingers to make a thin roll.

step 4 attach to spindle
Start to wrap the twisted piece around the bottom of the spool.

step 5 continue to twist
Continue to twist the paper in the same direction. Leave about 13 cm (5 in.) at the end to attach onto the next strip.

step 6 attach next strip
To attach the next strip, twist the start of strip 2 to the end of strip 1.

step 7 carry on
Continue twisting the strips together until you reach your desired length.

ABOVE *Red twiggy neckpiece* by
Sarah Keay, 2007. *Financial Times*
newspaper coated with a fine layer of
acrylic varnish.
Photograph © Fiona Wright.

RIGHT *Spun red FT bangle* by Sarah
Keay, 2006. *Financial Times*
newspaper coated with a fine layer of
acrylic varnish.
Photograph © Simon Armitt.

12 smocking

smocking bangle
by joanne haywood

EQUIPMENT REQUIRED

- dressmakers' chalk
- a soft brush
  (to brush away chalk)
- steel ruler
- sewing needle

MATERIALS REQUIRED

- a piece of acrylic felt
  measuring 60 cm x 14 cm
  (23.5 x 5.5 in.)
- red shearing elastic
- white cotton

VARIATION

Choose your own colour
variations. You might
want to choose blacks
and greys or contrasting
colours as I have.

This textile bangle makes reference to the traditional technique of smocking. Contrasting fabric and thread are used to create a soft sculptural form. Choose your own colour combination to design your own.

method

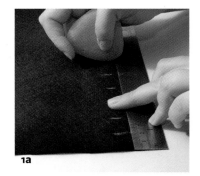

1a

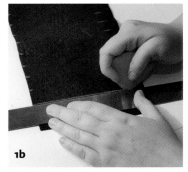

1b

step 1

Take your piece of felt and, with the dressmakers' chalk, mark 2 cm (0.8 in.) points along the 60 cm (23.5 in.) sides. Join the points together to create vertical lines.

2a

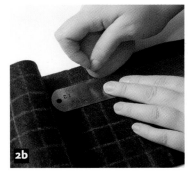

2b

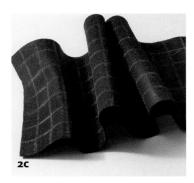

2c

step 2

Measure 2 cm (0.8 in.) points along the 14 cm (5.5 in.) edges and again join the points from each side together. If you are using a 30 cm

(12 in.) ruler, you will need to add some additional points as a guide as your ruler will not stretch across the 60 cm (23.5 in.).

3a

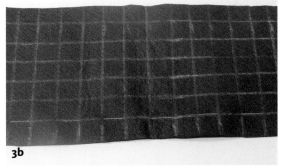

3b

step 3

Thread a 70 cm (27.5 in.) piece of white cotton onto the needle and insert it into the felt at the first square on the shorter side. Bring the thread

up at the point above it and again back in at the next point. Continue to do this all the way along the 60 cm (23.5 in.) stretch and then take the thread off the needle.

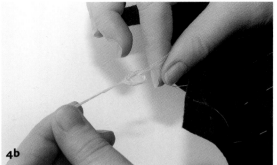

step 4

Repeat this process for each run of points and then knot the ends of the threads at one end.

step 5

Holding the threads at the loose end, push the fabric towards the tied end. It will pleat up and form a concertina shape. Knot the loose end together and cut away the excess cotton thread.

step 6

Take a length of red shearing elastic and pull through the first two folds of the fabric at one end. Use the elastic to fasten three knots and cut off the ends so you are left with a 5–7 mm (0.2–0.3 in.) tuft. Use the chalk lines as a guide.

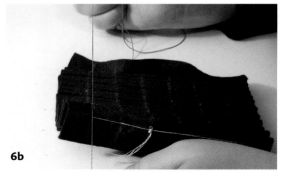

step 7

Knot the next two folds together and so on until you work along the whole line. The last knot will hold a single fold only. Start the next row and where you've knotted two folds in the first line, this time knot one fold to start with. On the second knot go back to knotting two folds and then two folds again to the end of the row. You will notice that you are joining alternate folds in each line which will create a V shape.

step 8

Carry on knotting the folds together and, after the third row, you will see a diamond formation taking place.

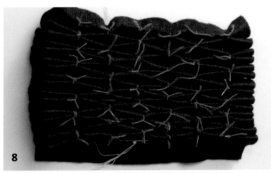

step 9

When you have knotted all the folds, cut away the white cotton and gently pull the felt apart to reveal more of the fold pattern. At this stage you can gently rub away the dressmakers' chalk with your fingers or a soft brush.

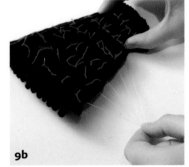

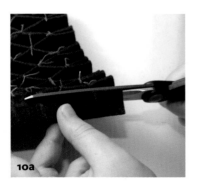

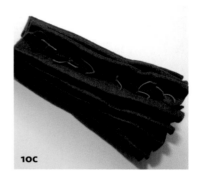

step 10

Cut any excess felt away from each short side and then join the two short sides together with your stitching on the inside. Knot the edges together where there are existing knots.

step 11

Fold the sides outwards so that both sides meet and you can see the knots again.

step 12

Knot along the open edges to join both sides. Knot every 2 cm. The natural folds will show you where to stitch. Stretch the shape from the centre to shape into a bangle and trim away any long or untidy strands of elastic.

Health & Safety

This project has no real health and safety implications, apart from working with sewing needles. It is suitable for everyone as it is fairly low-tech.

VARIATION

You could stitch beads into the surface with every knot or use a vintage patterned fabric instead of felt. All fabrics fold differently, felt keeps a good crisp edge, other fabrics may be too floppy, so always make a small test piece first.

VARIATION

Try stitching ribbon along the edge of the felt before pleating to add extra emphasis to the folds, or add surface detail with freehand embroidery, fabric paint or appliqué.

gallery – smocking

1	3	5	
2	4	6	7

1 *Pearl Abundance*, neckpiece, Uli Rapp, 2007. Silicone rubber, textiles, screen printing, magnet. 52 x 20 x 0.5 cm (20.5 x 8 x 0.2 in.). German, lives and works in The Netherlands.

2 *Cuff*, Loukia Richards, 2007. Textiles, threads, semi precious stones. 6 x 10 x 0.5 cm approx. (2 x 4 x 0.2 in.). Greece.

3 *Zeebauw*, necklace, Lucy Sarneel. Silver, ribbon, zinc, shells. 39.5 x 19 cm (15.5 x 7.5 in.). The Netherlands.

4 *Ring*, Kerstin Klux, 2007. Steel, silver, textile, silicon, glass, acrylic. Germany.

5 *Heirloom brooch*, Sharon Massey, 2006. Steel, cotton muslin, cameo. 12.5 x 10 x 2.5 cm (5 x 4 x 1 in.). USA.

6 *Silver Silk ring*, Shelby Fitzpatrick, 2001. Silver, pleated silk. 5 x 4 x 4 cm (2 x 1.5 x 1.5 cm). American, lives and works in England.

7 *Meta-Clothing*, Kyeok Kim, 2006. Leather, 18ct gold, sapphires, gold plated silver. Various sizes. Korea.

gallery – anna s. king

Anna. S. King is a renowned Scottish fibre artist who produces jewellery, baskets and large fibre installations. She combines traditional techniques with diverse materials ranging from silk and jute to nylon and plastic.

ABOVE *Japanese square braid plaited necklace*, 2006/2007. Recycled calendar.

RIGHT *Ostrich Feather Fronds*, 2006/2007. Ostrich feather fronds, pearl beads and antique lace.

Photographs © Anna King.

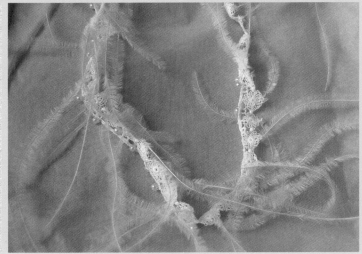

kathryn partington

Kathryn Partington is interested in the application of surface pattern and ornamentation within jewellery. She produces one-off wearable items whilst also utilising her background training in tableware, ceramics and printed textiles. The origin of her use of decoration comes from deconstructing and then reconstructing an 1890 Victorian adaptation of a Japanese style tableware pattern. The processes that she uses include hand drawing, engraving and slip casting.

"I re-create, evolve and reference the past, while the manipulations of my various processes contain echoes of the original that will always remain."
Kathryn Partington, 2007.

For *Ethereal 1 and 2*, Kathryn has screen-printed decoration upon various weights of silk, mainly sheer and lightweight. These are then connected and interlinked with handmade silver hoops.

TOP *Ethereal 1 neckpiece*, 2007. Metallic, flock, raised and foil pigments upon natural and dyed silks with silver.

RIGHT *Ethereal 2 neckpiece*, 2007. Connected silver hoops linked with sheer, dyed and natural silk.

Photographs © Kathryn Partington.

joanne haywood

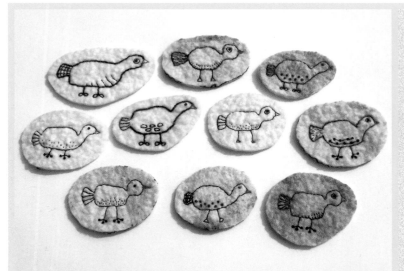

For this cute series of bird brooches, Joanne has used a variety of techniques, including felting and embroidery.

Bird Brooches, taken from *100 Oslo Brooches*, 2007. Hand felted brooches, stitched drawings and oxidised silver fastenings. Photograph © Joanne Haywood.

ABOVE *Bud Berry Bracelet*, 2007. Oxidised silver wire with textile bracelet.

LEFT *Cloudberry Neckpiece*, 2007. Cotton and felt. This stunning neckpiece is constructed with crocheted cotton with merino felt elements to give a dramatic effect.

Photographs © Joanne Haywood.

laila smith

STITCHED

"I use textile as I am interested in the processes in working it. The time needed to construct the pieces I use is central to the finished piece, the effort is reflected in the stitches seen. All the fabrics used are fragments of domestic textiles and family cloth. This use of textile that has had a previous life is central to my jewellery. The combination of textile and precious metals ensures a longevity to the work and somehow makes them more recognisable as jewellery."

Laila Smith, 2008.

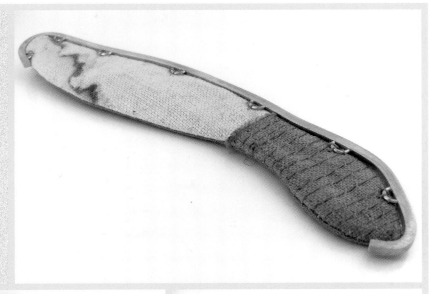

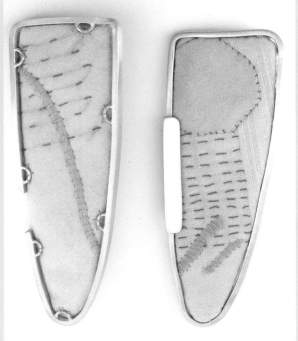

TOP *Textile brooch 1*, 2007. Silver and textile, hand stitch, machine stitch and jewellery techniques.

ABOVE *Textile brooch 2*, 2008. Silver and textile, hand stitch, machine stitch and jewellery techniques.

LEFT 2 *Brooches*, 2008. Silver and textile hand stitch, machine stitch and jewellery techniques.

Photographs © Laila Smith.

jimena rios

"Jewellery is inherited, given, saved, cared for, searched for. It's gathered, it's remembered.

Jewellery tells stories, it speaks of those who wore it. Jewellery communicated to others. It attracts and makes one think about the person who wears it. For these reasons jewellery is fascinating to me and when I am not making it, I look, search and find things which help me to tell my stories when I sit at my bench, in order to tell the stories of the pieces I make, once they are converted into jewellery belonging to others."

Jimena Rios, 2009.

RIGHT *Necklace*, 2004. Silver, fabric.

BELOW LEFT *My friend is a chicken*, 2004. Silver, fabric.

BELOW RIGHT *Solitaire single ring* 2008. Silver, fabric.

Photographs © Jimena Rios.

rita marcangelo

"Transformation has always fascinated me. The ability of changing the initial aspect of a given material, in this case silk, in order that it takes on a completely different aspect, is the idea behind this group of works. A metamorphosis of the texture of the material, but also the size, is achieved through burning techniques. I obtain different effects by means of changing the intensity of the heat.

Initially, I would burn the silk and then construct the rest of the piece around it, but I am now able to control the desired effect, so I usually think of the result I wish to achieve first and then proceed. The colours are accomplished with the use of acrylic paints." Rita Marcangelo, 2009.

CLOCKWISE FROM ABOVE LEFT
Ring, 2004. Silver, 18ct gold, burnt silk, acrylics.
Brooch, 2004. Silver, 18ct gold, burnt silk, acrylics.
All Wrapped Up, brooch, 2006. Silver, burnt silk.
Movimento, ring, 2009. Silver, burnt silk, acrylics.
Cloud 2, ring, 2009. Silver, burnt silk, acrylics.

Photographs © Rita Marcangelo

loukia richards

LEFT *Vintage lace cuff*, 2006. Vintage furniture textile, early 20th century handmade lace, pearls, vintage button, embroidery. 4.5 x 18 cm (1.7 x. 7 in.). A cuff made of various vintage fabrics.

Recent work inspired by the myth of labyrinth and by Greek embroidery motifs. I used the 'lego-game-principle'; the jewellery pieces are adjustable; the wearer can put as many pieces together as she wishes and form a necklace, a bracelet, a cuff, a pectoral etc. I wanted to encourage the wearer to play with my jewellery and to customise it according to her needs and thus become creative. The jewellery also intends to make (funny) allusions to iconic art treasures like the Mycenean gold collections of fifteenth century BC.

"*In the Greek culture, like in most ancient cultures, textile is a metaphor for life, thus a sacred material.*

Innumerable myths manifest the importance of textile in hellenic social and religious life.

The patron of ancient Athens and also patron of the crafts, Athena, the goddess of wisdom, was a weaver. At the most important festival of ancient Athens, Panathenea, young women devoted to the Virgin goddess carried a huge veil to her temple Parthenon. They had woven the veil for nine months. There, Athena's archaic statue, which the legend said had fallen from the sky, was enwrapped in the lengthy veil. The veil was carried to Acropolis raised as a sail on a T-formed mast, atop a chariot which looked like a ship.

This piece of textile was not only an allusion to the naval power of Athens, dominant in the seas, but more important, an allusion to the city – polis in Greek, hence politics, which ever since the archaic period was considered a 'ship' mastered by the crew of its citizens.

I work with textile because I am fascinated by the symbolism of the material. The jewellery I present is inspired by the decorative elements of the Cycladic, the Minoan and the Mycenean civilizations that prexisted classical Greece. These motifs represent mostly nature in abstraction. Nature is omnipresent in the aesthetics and religious beliefs of the archaic world. The conceptual accuracy and simplicity of the motifs is mesmerizing. It is fascinating that the pictorial representation of nature remains unchanged from archaic times to present day Greece on vases, embroideries, murals etc."

Loukia Richards, 2009.

RIGHT *Red deer, necklace,* 2008. (With adjustable deer pendant and buttonholes for adjusting additional ornaments.) Length: 40 cm (16 in.), red deer pendant: 7 x 12 cm (2.5 x 4.5 in.). Textile, silk and cotton threads and silver.

Inspired by a well known deer motif as well as archaic silver/gold techniques. The cord is inspired by the 'animal rope with holes' used in Kurdistan.

Inspired by Artemis's holy animal as well as by fifteenth century BC Mycenean gold and silver sheet jewellery techniques. Artemis was the goddess of Nature in the Greek world. According to Greek mythology, the Myceanean princess Iphigeneia, destined to be sacrificed to Artemis, was pitied by the goddess and replaced by a deer. This sacrifice enabled the Greek fleet to sail auspiciously to Troy. Red stands for the sacrificial blood.

The cord is inspired by the 'rope with holes' used for animals. The deer motif remains unchanged in Greek art from eigth century BC vase painting to eighteenth century AD embroidery.

LEFT *Balkan pectoral,* pectoral ornament, 2006. Textile, Ottoman empire silver coins, semi-precious stones, silk/cotton threads, vintage buttons. 50 x 23 cm. (19.5 x 9 in.).
Inspired by the richly decorated pectoral ornament or bustier, representative of the wearer's wealth and social status still worn in the Balkan peninsula.

hanna hedman

Enough Tears To Cry for Two

"I was told that time heals all wounds. I have tried to illustrate time in all my pieces by using repetition and time-consuming techniques. I have tried to compress or you can say preserve time into my work. Something that has taken great amount of time can be seen in just a moment.

I drill holes, I solder I repeat into tiresome.

I feel that grief has become more and more something hidden and that people don't want to show themselves as weak. We can only feel compassion and sympathy when we put ourselves in someone else's situation, but how is it possible to do so if we can't physically see or understand from their outside that the other person is suffering from grief? It is only when you show yourself to be grieving that others can feel sympathy.

I want grief to be made visible on the outside. I want the outside to mirror inside feelings.

Whether the loss was recent or long ago, it may still limit you to fully participate in life.

Most of my pieces of jewellery are difficult to wear and they limit you in your daily life in the same way as grief does. Some of them are heavy to carry, others are big or hurt you.

I use already defined symbols and combinations to make my pieces worn messages. I wanted to make the messages strange and in some cases surreal because that is what grief is to me; inner conflict of emotions that many times contradict each other. I work a lot by intuition, but also get some of my ideas from art of the past as I have looked closer and been inspired by the Victorian era during eighteenth century England. This was a period known for displaying inner feelings outwards, full of symbolism and an atmosphere of sadness. Jewellery during this time was commonly used during mourning in memory of a deceased person. The aesthetics from this period has motivated me and I believe that my work is an acknowledgement to this period.

My jewellery is inspired by grief and death, but I have also added aspects of regeneration and growth at the same time to give them hope.

The collection incorporates grief symbols such as teardrops, roots, numbers, and envelopes with a cold autumn atmosphere of withered tree branches.

Materials that are used are copper, silver, paint and synthetic fiber." Hanna Hedman, 2008.

Photographer: Sanna Lindberg.
Make-up: Ignacio Alonso.
Model: Oona Linke.

sally collins

"The main focus of my work lies in the exploration of the evolution of form and ornamentation. In my collection Make Do and Mend I have created a range of jewels from second-hand fabric, crochet, lace, heat treated copper and gold-plated elements. I aim to explore a traditionally domestic approach to recycling and sustainability, whilst following the progression of form and decoration through an evolution of scale, density and eccentricity.

I create wearable compositions through the layering of pattern, colour and form with an emphasis on excess detailing and frills, taking pleasure in unusual or abundant combinations of fabrics and textures. My jewellery strives to explore the concept of the 'Superfrilly' and ask the question, 'When is enough really enough?'" Sally Collins, 2008.

ABOVE *Reknitted (3)*. Brooch, 2008. Heat treated copper, gold-plated copper, fabric, nylon, wool. 12.5 x 10 x 3.5 cm (5 x 4 x 1.4 in.).

LEFT *Bridesmaids*. Brooch, 2008. Heat treated copper, gold-plated copper, fabric, cotton, paint. 16 x 16 x 3 cm (6 x 6 x 1 in.).

BELOW, LEFT TO RIGHT
Isabella. Brooch, 2008. Patinated copper, gold-plated copper, oxidised copper, sterling silver, fabric, paint, cotton. 13.5 x 11 x 5 cm (5 x 4 x 2 in.).
Cloud Busting. Brooch, 2008. Patinated copper, gold-plated copper, cotton. 8.5 x 7 x 2.5 cm (3.5 x 2.5 x 1 in.).
Tartan Party. Brooch, 2008. Heat treated copper, gold-plated copper, fabric, lace, paint. 8.5 x 9 x 4 cm (3.5 x 3.55 x 1.5 in.).

Photographs © Sally Collins.

keren cornelius

Keren Cornelius' work is inspired by the repertory costumes of the Royal Opera House. Enduring a harsh cycle of storage, laundering and wear, these garments are painstakingly repaired, patched and darned. Over time, new layers of thread are entwined with old, creating intricate patterns across the surface of the fabric. Patches overlap imperfections and rows of tiny holes trace former stitch lines. The result is an ongoing dialogue of exchange between maker, wearer, restorer and garment.

Within this jewellery collection, some pieces represent the entwined layers of stitching; in others the stitches are barely visible, but subtly change the colour of the surface of the pieces. Referring to the labour involved in the restoration process, each piece is titled according to the duration of its construction, or the quantity of thread used. Each wearer adds their own personal story to an increasingly rich tapestry of exchange and response, construction and erosion.

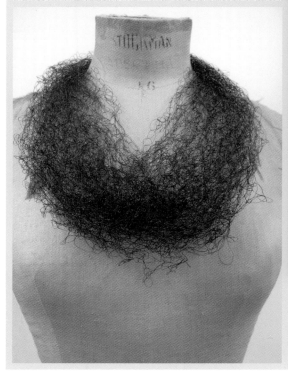

ABOVE *48 hours*, embroidery thread.

LEFT *5.5 hours*, metallic thread.

Photographs © Keren Cornelius.

sarah keay

"The utilisation of unconventional objects, juxtaposed with precious materials allows my jewellery to continually develop and diversify, whilst the ancient technique of hand bobbin knitting questions the traditional roles of jewellery and its perceptions. It questions the subject of jewellery, teasing out our relationships with it: what we wear and why we wear it. The 'unique value' associated with jewellery, be it intrinsic, inherent, perceived or added to jewellery through the owning and wearing of it, informs my recent work and is the basis for further research."
Sarah Keay, 2008.

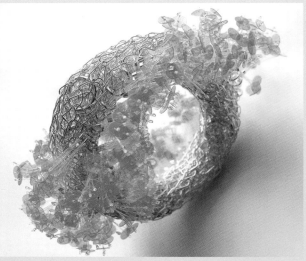

ABOVE *Silver bangle*, 2008. Sterling silver, plastic, monofilament, enamel.

LEFT *Ruby bangle*, 2008. 9ct gold, gold-plated silver, rolled gold, rubies, monofilament, enamel.

Photographs © Sarah Keay.

jeehyun chung

"As a Korean, I wish to reflect my Korean heritage in my jewellery.

Having lived in Edinburgh for four years, I have become inspired to combine the traditional elements of my culture with western modern aesthetic.

Delicacy and repetition in structures fascinates me. I have been particularly influenced by the kind of structures found in traditional Korean accessories and flower patterns and the skeletal frames of scaffolding and try to explore a wide variety of materials and colours.

These ideas have inspired me to create jewellery using multiple layers and repeating frames."

Jeehyun Chung, 2008.

ABOVE LEFT *Repetition ring*, 2008. Oxidised silver, Korean silk, thread.

ABOVE RIGHT *Repetition flower bracelet*, 2008. Oxidised silver, Korean silk, thread.

LEFT *Repetition flower earrings*, 2008. Silver, Korean silk, thread.

Photographs © Jeehyun Chung and John K McGregor.

Pearl bangle by Sarah Keay, 2008. Sterling silver, pearls, monofilament, enamel. Photograph © Sarah Keay.

other quick tips

HOW TO LOOP THE ENDS OF WIRE

Hold the wire firmly at the tip using a pair of round-nose pliers. slowly twist the wire starting at 12 o'clock, turn to 3 o'clock, turn pliers back to 12 and repeat until you have a very tight loop. If necessary flatten and straighten loop with a pair of flat pliers.

HOW TO JOIN TWO ENDS OF WIRE

The easiest way to join two wires together is to twist them together. Make sure to file down the ends of both wires so that they don't catch. You can also make a feature of the join. Experiment with looping the ends into one another or even try elaborate twisting and looping.

HOW TO MAKE YOUR OWN JUMP LINKS

Choose a strong piece of rod the diameter that you require your jump links, e.g. a piece of dowling, or steel tube. Tightly coil the wire around the rod. Remove the spring from the rod. The neatest way to cut the links is to use a jewellers piercing saw, however, if the wire is thin enough ordinary scissors can be just as good. To close the link, use a pair of flat-nosed pliers and gently twist the ends until they join up perfectly.

Neon Yellow bangle by Sarah Keay, 2008. Sterling silver, plastic, monofilament, enamel. Photograph © Sarah Keay.

list of suppliers

BEADS

The Bead Shop
21a Tower Street,
Covent Garden
London
WC2H 9NS, UK
telephone: 020 7240 0931
sales@beadworks.co.uk
www.beadworks.co.uk
The shop is on two floors and
stocks a vast range of beads
from Swarovski crystals to semi-
precious beads.

Mailorder Beads
Market Street
Nottingham
NG1 6HY, UK
telephone: 011595 88899
fax: 0115 9588903
General enquiries:
info@mailorder-beads.co.uk
Order enquiries :
orders@mailorder-beads.co.uk
www.mailorder-beads.co.uk
Stockists of a wide range of
beads, crystals, findings,
accessories, tools and
magazines. The shop also runs
beading workshops.

Kernowcraft Rocks & Gems
Ltd Bolingey
Perranporth
Cornwall
TR6 0DH, UK
telephone: 01872 573888
Fax: 01872 573704
info@kernowcraft.com
www.kernowcraft.com

Supplies everything from
natural gems and crystals to
tools, findings and a large range
of semi-precious beads.

21st Century Beads
Unit 11,
County Workshops,
Wood St,
Dewsbury,
West Yorkshire,
WF13 1QU, UK
telephone: 01924 452252
www.beadmaster.com
Suppliers of loose beads and
jewellery-making materials to
the public and trade.

JEWELLERY TOOLS, EQUIPMENT AND MATERIALS
Baird & Co

Glasgow branch:
82 Mitchell Street
Glasgow
Lanarkshire
G1 3NA, UK
telephone: 0141 248 5646

London branch:
137 High Street
London
E15 2RB, UK
telephone: 020 8555 5217
Bullion merchants.

Bellore
39 Greville Street
London
EC1N 8PJ, UK
telephone: 020 7404 3220
fax: 020 7404 3221
order@bellore.co.uk
www.bellore.co.uk
Major supplier of semi-
precious beads and stones,
findings, tools and machinery.

Cookson Precious Metals
59-83 Vittoria Street
Birmingham,
B1 3NZ , UK
telephone: 0845 100 1122 or
0121 200 2120
fax: 0121 212 6456
birmingham.sales@cooksongol
d.com
www.cooksongold.com
The UK's largest 'one stop
shop' for the jewellery trade.
Offers over 10,000 products
including a wide choice of
wires, findings and chains.

HS Walsh & Sons Ltd
243 Beckenham Road
Beckenham
Kent
BR3 4TS, UK
telephone: 020 8778 7061
www.hswalsh.com
Supply a great range of
jewellery and watchmaking
tools and equipment.

Rashbel
24-28 Hatton Wall
London
EC1N 8JH, UK
telephone: 020 7831 5646
order@rashbel.com
www.rashbel.com
Suppliers of semi-precious
stones, precious metal clay,
gold and silver leaves,
decorative strips and tools.

Wires.co.uk
18 Raven Road
South Woodford
London E18 1HW, UK
telephone: 020 8505 0002
fax: 020 8559 1114
dan@wires.co.uk
www.wires.co.uk
Sub division of the Scientific
Wire Company. Suppliers of an
extensive range of wires for all
types of craft. Also has an online
craftwork gallery showcasing
makers work. Supply gold,
silver and enamelled wires on
50g-500g spools.

YARNS
Wingham Wool Work
70 Main St
Wentworth
Rotherham
South Yorkshire
S62 7TN, UK
telephone: 01226 742926
fax: 01226 741166
wingwool@clara.net
www.winghamwoolwork.co.uk
The largest supplier of fibres for
hand spinning, felt making and
textile crafts in the UK.

OTHER
Arduino
www.arduino.cc
Good website for info/blogs on
other projects. Order Arduino
products and learn more about
programming. Download the
programming environment.

Caurnie
The Organic Herb Garden
Canal Lane
Kirkintilloch
Scotland G66 1QZ, UK
telephone:0141 776 1218
Sales@caurnie.com
www.caurnie.com
Specialists in cold process
vegan soaps and cleansing
products.

**Central Scotland Lacemaking
Supplies**
3 Strude Howe
Alva
Clackmannanshire
FK12 5JU, UK
telephone: 01259 762523
hazel@csls.co.uk
www.csls.co.uk
Offer a wide range of supplies
from lace making pillows to
patterns, accessories and books.

Conductive Steel Thread
Lame Lifesaver
Robert Smith
2039 Cedar Hill Cross Road
Victoria BC
Canada V8P 2R5
Initially for repairing lame for
fencing, the thread can be
utilised in many other ways.

Fred Aldous Ltd
37 Lever Street
Manchester
England M1 1LW, UK
telephone: 0161 236 4224
www.fredaldous.co.uk
Offers over 25,000 different
products for art and craft
projects.

John Lewis Department Stores
Stores Nationwide telephone:
0845 049 049
www.johnlewis.com
Fantastic high street
haberdashery department for a
wide range of crafts including
jewellery, knitting and
embroidery.

Maplin Electronics
telephone: 0870 429 6000
customercare@maplin.co.uk
www.maplin.co.uk
Maplins in the UK supply basic
electronic components,
breadboarding kits and
multimeters.

bibliography

Amulets: A world of secret powers, charms and magic by Sheila Paine published by Thames and Hudson Ltd
ISBN: 0-500-28510-1
A fantastic book that documents amulets throughout the ages from their symbolic meanings to their protective functions.

Jewelry: From Antiquity to Present by Clare Phillips published by Thames and Hudson
ISBN: 0-500-20287-7
Fascinating and informative guide to the development of jewellery throughout history.

Tone Vigeland: Jewellery and Sculpture Movements in Silver by Cecilie Malm Brundtland published by Arnoldsche
ISBN: 3-89790-185-4
A fantastic and inspiring book about one of the worlds leading contemporary jewellers. Tone Vigeland's work is absolutely gorgeous.

Necklaces and Pendants by Angie Boothroyd published by A & C Black
ISBN: 978-0-7136-7933-5
Great book from A & C Black's handbook series. Has projects as varied as french knitting through to enamelling and Japanese lacquer.

Wire Jewellery by Hans Stofer published by A & C Black
ISBN: 978-0-7136-6634-2
Lovely book concentrating solely on working with wire. Also has a great range of makers pages with images.

Textile Techniques in Metal by Arline M. Fisch published by Robert Hale Limited
ISBN: 0-7090-6007-6
The Bible for anyone who wants to learn more about how to manipulate metal into textile techniques. Very authoritative and inspiring.

North American Indian Jewelry and Adornment: from prehistory to the present by Lois Sherr Dubin published by Harry N. Abrams, Inc
ISBN: 0-8109-3689-5

further reading

Physical Computing by Dan O'Sullivan and Tom Igoe published by Thomson Course Technology
ISBN: 1-59200-346
A book for those who wish to learn more about how to utilise electronics within their work.

Jewelry Concepts and Technology by Oppi Untracht published by Robert Hale Limited
ISBN: 0-7091-9616-4
A huge bible of all jewellery techniques.
A brilliant book for anyone who wants to learn how to make their jewellery.

Crocheted Wire Jewelry: Innovative Designs and Projects by Leading Artists by Arline M Fisch published by Lark Books
ISBN: 978-1-5799-0660-3
Another book from Arline Fisch. This is a great step by step book for anyone who wants to learn more.

Elegant Fantasy: The Jewelry of Arline Fisch by David McFadden, Ida Rigby and Robert Bell published by Arnoldsche
ISBN: 978-3-9253-6901-8
Inspiring book showing how knitted wire can be so beautiful. Documents Fisch's work through small pieces to large scale neckpieces.

Creative Recycling in Embroidery by Val Holmes published by Batsford Ltd
ISBN: 978-0-7134-8986-6
Covers both hand and machine embroidery techniques along with how to utilise recycled materials into something beautiful.

Paper Textiles by Christina Leitner published by A & C Black Publishers Ltd
ISBN: 978-0-7136-7444-6
This book covers the history of paper textiles through to techniques and projects that incorporate a variety of textile techniques to create a range of items.

Three Dimensional Embroidery by Janet Edmonds published by Batsford Ltd
ISBN: 978-0-7134-8965-1
How to construct 3D textile projects, including boxes, spheres and cylinders.

Fusing Fabric: Cutting, Bonding and Mark making with the Soldering Iron by Margaret Beal published by Batsford Ltd
ISBN: 978-0-7134-9068-8
A really original technique, using an iron to bond fabrics!

Stitch, Dissolve, Distort in Machine Embroidery by Maggie Grey and Valerie Campbell-Harding published by Batsford Ltd
ISBN: 978-0-7134-8996-5
Various techniques on how to dissolve, melt and manipulate fabrics.

Felt to Stitch: Creative Felting for Textile Artists by Sheila Smith published by Batsford Ltd
ISBN: 978-0-7134-9008-4
A good range for all abilities in surface embellishment, particularly for those who want to develop their feltmaking techniques.

Paper, Metal and Stitch by Maggie Grey and Jane Wild published by Batsford Ltd
ISBN: 978-0-7134-8918-7
How to manipulate paper and how to utilise metals such as wires and foils, within crafts.

Jewellers: the directory by The Association for Contemporary Jewellery published by A & C Black Publishers Ltd
ISBN: 978-0-7136-8409-4
Directory from the Association for Contemporary Jewellery showing makers work and their contact details.

Jewellery Making: techniques book by Elizabeth Olver published by Apple Press
ISBN: 1-840923-36-9
Another good book for those wishing to learn how to make their own metal jewellery.

Flora Necklaces, by Emma Gale. 2006. crochet mohair flowers, 18ct yellow gold, pearls, silk ribbon and citrine beads. Photograph by Graham Clark.

websites

www.acj.org.uk
Website for the Association for Contemporary Jewellery.

www.alloyjewellers.org.uk/publicdirectory.php
Alloy is a Herefordshire based group of jewellers and silversmiths. Their public directory lists a large variety of contact details from material suppliers to workshops.

www.alternatives.it
Alternatives is a fantastic jewellery gallery in the historic centre of Rome. Run by Rita Marcangelo it stocks a wide range of contemporary jewellers work.

www.axisweb.org
Axis is an online resource about contemporary art. It has a wide range of profiles of professional artists and makers.

www. craftscotland.org
Craftscotland represents and promotes contemporary Scottish craft. You can search for makers' profiles, galleries and workshops.

www.feliekevanderleest.com
Felieke van der Leest combines found objects, such as plastic toy animals, crochet work and gold and silver elements into her pieces of jewellery.

www.florabook.com
Flora Book's ornamental body pieces cross the boundaries between garments and jewellery.

www.klimt02.net
Showcasing contemporary jewellers from around the world, lists galleries dedicated to jewellery and the latest exhibitions.

www.photostore.org.uk
Photostore was set up by the Crafts Council to profile contemporary craft makers from across the UK.

places to visit

UNITED KINGDOM
Contemporary Applied Arts
2 Percy Street
London W1
telephone: 020 7436 2344
fax: 020 7490 0556
mail info@caa.org.uk
www.caa.org.uk

National Museums of Scotland
Chambers Street
Edinburgh EH1 1JF
telephone: 0131 225 7534
www.nms.ac.uk

Victoria and Albert Museum
V&A South Kensington
Cromwell Road
London SW7 2RL
telephone: 020 7942 2000
www.vam.ac.uk

Lesley Craze Gallery
33 - 35a Clerkenwell Green
London EC1R 0DU
telephone: 020 7608 0393
fax: 020 7251 5655
info@lesleycrazegallery.co.uk
www.lesleycrazegallery.co.uk

USA
Julie Artisans Gallery
762 Madison Avenue
NY 10021 New York
www.julieartisans.com

Charon Kransen Arts
456 West 25th Street
NY 10001

New York, USA
telephone: (212) 627 5073
fax: (212) 633 9026
chakran@earthlink.net
www.charonkransenarts.com

Helen Drutt
1721 Walnut Street
PA 19103
Philadelphia, USA
telephone: (215) 735 1625
fax: (215) 732 1382
www.helendrutt.com

Jewelers' Werk Galerie
3319 Cady's Alley
NW 20007
Washington DC, USA
telephone: (202) 337-3319
ellen@jewelerswerk.com
www.jewelerswerk.com

Mobilia Gallery
358 Huron Avenue
MA 02138
Cambridge, USA
telephone: (617) 876 2109
fax: (617) 876 2110
mobiliaart@aol.com
www.mobilia-gallery.com

Velvet da Vinci
2015 Polk Street
CA 94109
San Francisco, USA
telephone: (415) 441 0109
fax: (415) 386 2492
info@velvetdavinci.com
www.velvetdavinci.com

NETHERLANDS
Galerie Louise Smit
Prinsengracht 615
1016 HT
Amsterdam, Netherlands
telephone: 0031 020 625 98 98
fax: 0031 020 428 02 16

Galerie Marzee
Lage Markt 3
Waalkade 4 6511 VK,
Nijmegen, Netherlands
telephone: 0031 024 3229670
fax: 0031 024 3604688
mail@marzee.nl
www.marzee.nl

Galerie Ra Vijzelstraat
80 1017 HL,
Amsterdam, Netherlands
telephone: 0031 020 6265100
fax: 0031 020 6204595
mail@galerie-ra.nl
www.galerie-ra.nl

Galerie Rob Koudijs
Elandsgracht 12
1016TV
Amsterdam, Netherlands
telephone: 0031 020 331 87 96
info@galerierobkoudijs.nl
www.galerierobkoudijs.nl

ITALY
Alternatives
Via d'Ascanio, 19
(Via della Scrofa)
00186
Roma

glossary of terms

Angelina fibre is an unusual fibre that comes in iridescent, holographic and metalized colours. It can either be heat bonded, using an iron and greaseproof paper, to make sheets for use in decorative projects or felted in small quantities into fleece to add sparkle and colour.

Awl a tool with a long pointed spike used for punching holes or engraving surfaces.

Clasp The method of closing a necklace or bracelet.

Drawing wire the technique in which metal wire is pulled through the tapered holes of a drawplate to make them thinner or shaped, ranging from round to square.

Epoxy adhesive strong glues for wood, metal, glass, stone, and some plastics. They can be made flexible or rigid, transparent or opaque, coloured, fast setting or extremely slow setting.

Findings jewellery components such as jump rings, brooch backs and necklace clasps are all classed as findings.

Flock process in which small powdered fibres are applied to surfaces to give a texture like velvet.

Forged one of the most ancient metalworking processes where metal is shaped using an anvil and hammer.

Heddles a heddle is an integral part of a loom. Each thread in the warp passes through a heddle, which is used to separate the warp threads for the passage of the weft.

Jump link a small circle of wire used to link small jewellery elements together.

Mandrel a large tapered tool usually made from steel or wood that is used to form rings and bangles.

Rivets/riveting rivets are one of the oldest and most reliable types of fasteners, having been found in archaeological finds dating back to the Bronze Age. Solid rivets consist simply of a shaft and head which are secured with a hammer or rivet gun.

Silk cocoons the empty cocoons made by the mulberry silkworm larvae. These can be bought in a raw state that need cleaning or ready to use and available in bright dyed colours.

Silver metallic element with the symbol Ag. Usually alloyed with copper to create sterling silver.

Silver plated process where a thin layer of silver is adhered onto a metal surface.

Solder the joining of two metals by melting a metal alloy.

Sterling silver alloy of 92.5% silver and usually 7.5% copper.

Thread a type of yarn made for sewing by hand or machine.

Yarn a long continuous length of interlocked fibre's, for use in the production of textiles, sewing, crocheting, knitting, weaving, embroidery and ropemaking.

glossary of other textile techniques

Listed below are a brief range of the other most common textile techniques, arranged in alphabetical order. The Latin word for textile means 'to weave, braid or construct'. The simplest technique to master is felt making, which is to use heat and moisture to bind animal fibres together. Most of the other techniques begin with twisting, spinning or manipulating fibres together to make a yarn, thread if thin and rope if thick. This yarn can then be knitted, woven etc. There are also the techniques that are used as a form of embellishment, such as lace, embroidery and many forms of needlework.

Finally there are the construction techniques which include knitting and crochet.

Some of the techniques are very ancient. For instance knitted and woven fabrics appeared in the Middle East during the late stone age. From then until now these techniques have been continually developed into new meanings and items.

Many of these techniques fell into decline with the dawn of the Industrial Revolution, however nowadays, with the current trend towards crafts, most have gained a new resurgence.

Appliqué sewing one material on top of another.

Beadwork the embroidering, or loom weaving of beads, usually small glass seed beads. Glass bead embroidery has two stitches – overlay stitch and lazy stitch. Loomed beadwork requires a frame to support the warp and weft threads.

Binding both a noun and a verb in sewing to refer to finishing a seam or hem of a garment. A binding knot is a knot that may be used to keep an object or multiple loose objects together, using a string or a rope that passes at least once around them.

Braid, or **plait** a structure or pattern formed by intertwining strands of material such as wool or wire. Compared to weaving which needs a warp and weft, a braid is usually long and narrow and zigzag in form. The simplest possible braid is a flat, solid three-strand structure. More complicated braiding can be made, from usually an odd number of strands, to create a wider range of structures: wider ribbon-like bands, hollow or solid cylindrical cords. Braids are commonly used to make ropes.

Embroidery to decorate fabric or other materials with designs stitched in strands of thread or yarn using a needle. Embroidery may also use other media such as metal strips, pearls, beads and sequins. Examples of embroidery have been found from ancient Egypt and Iron Age Northern Europe. There are variations in technique depending upon the country of origin.

There are other varieties of techniques including: **surface embroidery**, where patterns are worked on top of the foundation fabric using decorative stitches and laid threads; **canvas work**, where threads are stitched through a fabric mesh to create a dense pattern that completely covers the initial fabric. An important difference between canvas work and surface embroidery is that surface work needs an embroidery hoop or frame to stretch the material and ensure even stitching tension to prevent the pattern from distorting. **Machine embroidery**, where designs are stitched by a sewing or specialist embroidery machine.

Lace lace making is an ancient craft. Referred to as an open-work fabric, it is patterned with open holes throughout the work and can be produced by both machine or by hand. The holes can be formed by the removal of certain threads or cloth from a previously woven fabric, but more often open spaces are created as part of the lace fabric. Traditionally linen, silk, gold, or silver threads were used. More recently lace is made with cotton thread. There are many types of lace, these include: **needle lace** made using a needle and thread. This is the most flexible of the lace-making processes. While some types can be made more quickly than the finest of bobbin laces, others are very time-consuming. **Cutwork** or **whitework**; lace constructed by removing threads from a woven background, and the remaining threads wrapped or filled with embroidery.

Macramé is another form of textile-making using knotting. Its primary knots are the square knot and forms of hitching. It has been used by sailors, especially in elaborate or ornamental knotting forms to decorate anything from knife handles to bottles to parts of ships. Common materials used in macramé include cotton twine, hemp, leather or yarn. Macramé is believed to have originated with 13th-century Arab weavers who knotted the excess thread and yarn along the edges of hand-loomed fabrics into decorative fringes on bath towels, shawls, and veils.

Needle felt special barbed felting needles that are generally used in industrial felting machines are used as a sculpting tool. By using a single needle or a small group of needles (2-5) in a hand held tool, these needles are used to sculpt the wool fibre. The barbs catch the fibre and push them through the layers of wool binding them together much like the wet felting process. Fine detail can be achieved using this technique and it is popular for 3D felted work.

Plying process used to create a strong and stable yarn. It is done by taking two or more strands of yarn that each have a twist to them and putting them together. The strands are then twisted together in the opposite direction from that in which they were spun.

Quillwork the ancient technique of weaving or sewing dyed and flattened porcupine quills. Method is unique to North American Indians.

Sewing is the stitching of cloth, leather or other materials, using a needle and thread. Its use is nearly universal among human populations and dates back to Palaeolithic times (30,000 BC). Sewing is the foundation for many needlework arts such as appliqué, canvas work, and patchwork.

Spinning an ancient textile art in which plant, animal or synthetic fibres are twisted together to form yarn. For thousands of years, fibres were spun by hand using a spindle and distaff. In the early medieval era the spinning wheel increased the output of individual spinners, and mass-production only began in the 18th century with the beginning of the Industrial Revolution. When spinning fleece into yarn, you must first wash the fleece, remove the dirt, card or comb it, and then spin it into singles. These singles are then used to create the finished yarn in a process known as **plying**. The purpose of plying singles is to strengthen them so that they do not break while knitting or crocheting them.

Flora Necklace by Emma Gale. 2008, crochet mohair flower, 18ct yellow gold, faceted red jasper beads, pearls, frosted citrine beads and silk ribbon. Photograph by Sallie Temple.

index

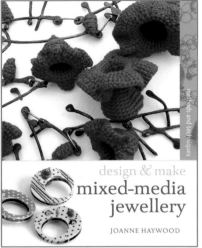

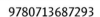

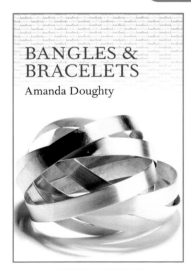
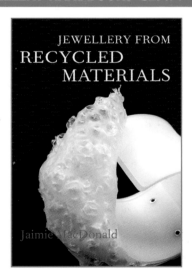
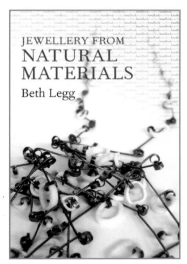